The
Disreputable
Profession

The Disreputable Profession

The Actor in Society

MENDEL KOHANSKY

Contributions in American Studies, Number 72

Greenwood Press
Westport, Connecticut • London, England

Library of Congress Cataloging in Publication Data

Kohansky, Mendel, 1911-1982
   The disreputable profession.

   (Contributions in American studies, ISSN 0084-9227 ;
no. 72)
   Bibliography: p.
   Includes index.
   1. Acting—History. 2. Theater and society.
I. Title. II. Series.
PN2061.K6 1984   792'.028'09   83-12807
ISBN 0-313-23824-3 (lib. bdg.)

Library of Congress Catalog Card Number: 83-12807
ISBN: 0-313-23824-3
ISSN: 0084-9227

First published in 1984

Greenwood Press
A division of Congressional Information Service, Inc.
88 Post Road West
Westport, Connecticut 06881

Printed in the United States of America

10 9 8 7 6 5 4 3 2 1

To Rolly

Contents

Preface

The Disreputable Profession is being published posthumously. The author, Mendel Kohansky, was a noted writer and theatre critic. It was his intention to show in this book that actors throughout history have been treated as a group apart, with a mixture of contempt and awe—placed at the bottom of some societies in the same categories as thieves and prostitutes and denied religious and civic rights, while in others they were regarded as practicing a legitimate profession. But the basic attitudes toward the profession, both social and cultural, remain the same, rooted in an unchangeable social psychology.

The author's interest in the theatre and respect for those associated with the profession—actors, teachers, directors, writers, critics, and most of all, the audiences—inspired him to devote many years of his life to the research required in preparing this work. Unfortunately, he passed away while completing the notes and bibliography. While every effort has been made to fill in the gaps he left, the possibility exists that in some cases sources, authors, publishers, or page numbers may have been omitted inadvertently. Since much of the research was done in American, British, and European libraries, museums, and archives, the omissions indicate that I was unable to track down the information here in Israel, in spite of my attempts to do so. I beg the indulgence of the reader and any source if such an error of omission does exist and apologize for it.

Because of the regrettable circumstances, I also apologize for my inability to mention by name all of the persons who had provided my late husband with assistance and gave so generously of their time and resources. I hope they will accept my sincere and grateful thanks for their contributions. I specifically thank the librarians of the theatre and museum archives of the Lincoln Center for the Performing Arts, New York; and the librarians of the American embassy's United States Information Service, the British Council, the Israel Film Archives Center, and Tel Aviv University—all in Tel Aviv, Israel.

I was fortunate in being able to call upon several people whose friendship, guidance, encouragement, and assistance enabled me to complete my task: Dr. Uri Rapp of the Departments of Sociology and Theatre, Tel Aviv University; Professor Don Rubin of the Department of Drama, York University, Ontario, and editor of *Canadian Theatre Review*; and Dr. Robert W. Walker, American Studies Program, George Washington University. Thank you all.

I wish also to express my appreciation and gratitude to the editors of Greenwood Press for their understanding in and contribution to seeing this important work printed.

Rolly King Kohansky
Tel Aviv, Israel

The
Disreputable
Profession

Introduction

It is a most unholy trade!

Henry James

Hamlet is dead, pierced by Laertes's sword, and four captains carry the body out, as a flight of angels sing the sweet prince on his way. Minutes later he is back on the stage bowing to a cheering audience, followed by the king and the queen, all of whom were dead. The audience, still moved by the awful carnage, applauds the live actors, thus accepting the fact that the events which a while ago so profoundly stirred their emotions were mere fiction, that they had voluntarily accepted illusion as reality, and that they are grateful to the actors for granting them this experience.

How grateful are they?

Thespis, the Greek who originated tragic drama, was visited one evening after a performance by the Athenian statesman and law-giver Solon. After complimenting the actor, the great man asked: "Aren't you ashamed to tell so many lies before so many people?" Thespis defended himself, arguing that after all it was nothing but play, but Solon would not accept it. Striking the floor with his staff, he cried: "Ah, if we honor such play as this, we shall find it some day in our daily business."[1]

Thus, at the very birth of the art of acting a wise man expressed the fear that has haunted society ever since, the fear that the actor with his power to create an illusory reality on the stage, with his gift for stirring our emotions, for making us experience vicarious terror and pity, constitutes a danger to the established order of things. How real is the power of the king if a commoner possessed of this skill can pretend to be one so convincingly? How real is the grief we feel over the loss of someone we loved if an actor can suffer so profoundly over the death of a fictitious person?

After the performance of the strolling players at Elsinore Castle, Hamlet reflects: how "monstrous" it is that a player should be able with such power and conviction to convey suffering for the fictitious Hecuba, "and all this for nothing! . . . What's Hecuba to him, or he to Hecuba, that he should weep for her?"

And Jean-Jacques Rousseau, writing at a time when the French theatre had attained its loftiest plateau, expressed his resentment in much stronger though less inspired words: "What is the art of the actor?", he angrily asked. "It is the art of counterfeiting himself, of putting on another character than his own . . . of forgetting his own place by dint of taking another's."[2]

Rousseau's contemptuous dismissal of the validity of the actor's art, and Hamlet's resentful affirmation of the actor's power, stem from the same source: the fear one experiences in the presence of the magic power the actor exercises over our emotions. The intensity and purity of the joy and the suffering of the love and the hatred emanating from the stage, seem to be so much greater than that of the emotions we experience in real life, and constitute a source of delight while posing questions we fear to answer.

Psychology provides some clues to the nature of the actor's power. Otto Fenichel believes that the actor whose psyche is a repository of a variety of subconscious sinful desires, the same as anyone else's, is possessed by an invincible urge to exhibit those desires in public, under the guise of the fictitious person he portrays. By gaining the audience's approval as expressed in applause, he expiates his guilt for harboring them. "A good actor actually reveals himself," Fenichel states. "He cannot play an emotion he has not experienced. The good actor *believes* that he plays his parts, but actually plays himself." And in doing so he has to elicit the participation of the public. "It is the unconscious aim of all acting to make the audience feel the same emotions that the actor displays. The spectators go to the theatre with the tacitly acknowledged intention of identifying themselves with the actors' portrayals. . . . The actor seeks to induce the audience's participation and approval of the commission of deeds which he, under the guise of pretense, would like to commit. If he succeeds, he feels less guilty."[3]

Thus the actor assumes the social role of the sacrificial goat who takes upon himself the spectator's uncommitted sins. As such he inspires both gratitude for lifting the burden of sin off the spectator's shoulders, and for assuming the revulsion one feels toward the sinner.

This would explain why actors need an audience in order to do their best acting. In rehearsals they perform mechanically, paying the most attention to technique and the externals of performing, while the inner force is missing. Theatre lore has it that a poor dress rehearsal portends a great opening night. What this means in rational terms is that the actors, who at rehearsal were doing little more than mouthing their lines and going through the motions, came to life when they were facing a hushed, expectant audience.

Fenichel's theory would also tend to explain the irresistible passion for acting that afflicts aspirants to the profession, a passion stronger than that experienced by candidates for any other calling, and of such singularity that in English a special term had to be coined for it. We speak of young men and women being "stage-struck." When deciding to become actors, usually against parental advice, they know that they have chosen an occupation which at worst is disreputable, and at best does not have full social approval, where success is always doubtful and seldom lasting; a profession that, in addition, is cruelly demanding, requiring of the practitioner a continued physical and emotional effort of a kind no other calling does.

The passion for exhibiting one's emotions in front of an audience is not, of course, the sole qualification for being an actor; one also needs the complex of gifts and skills that go under the general name of talent. One of the most important of these is the ability to watch one's own performance with a cool intelligence, to direct and check the passions one expresses so they do not get out of hand and turn a theatrical performance into a copy of life, that is, something trivial. Henry Irving is reported to have said that an actor who loses himself in his part will soon lose his audience. David Belasco illustrated the actor's ability to keep a cool head while passion tears his breast with the story of Tommasco Salvini, the Italian actor who in 1866 toured America playing Othello. On the last night of the fabulously successful long tour, he spoke his final line "no way but this, killing myself to die upon kiss," and plunging the dagger in his breast, collapsed on the dead Desdemona's couch, whispering to her "for the hundred and third and last time this season."[4]

The man (the woman appeared rather late on the stage) who exposes himself and thus exposes the audience, who makes us experience terror and pity while himself keeping a cool head, has always and everywhere, across the boundaries of nations and history, found himself in a socially ambivalent position. Like the priest in primitive society, he inspires both reverence for his supernatural powers, and fear for possessing them. Unlike the priest, however, he is not part of the social system—ancient Greece being a notable exception—and society has kept him at arm's length. His position has over the centuries ranged from utter rejection, which relegated him to the lowest social stratum, to the present-day celebrity of stars. However, though he may now lead an orderly and fairly affluent life in contrast to the hungry, ragged vagabonds of centuries ago, he still remains on the margin of society, the honors accorded to some outstanding individuals notwithstanding.

Under the gloss of public acceptance, the image of the actor as a sinister being on the one hand, and a person not to be taken seriously on the other, still persists. Boris Pasternak's celebrated hero Dr. Zhivago goes for a walk one evening with his friend "the actor and gambler" Constantin Illarionovich *Satan*idi. And in 1966, when the former actor Ronald Reagan was elected governor of California, the *New Statesman* of London published an article expressing indignation at an actor assuming a position of such importance. Richard West wrote:

> There are many reasons for regret at the news that Ronald Reagan has won the governorship of California. He is a great reactionary. He is a dullard. He is also an actor. . . . For many years the simple mummer has taken upon himself the role of sage, statesman and leader. Actresses in his country are recognized as leading spokesmen on South Africa, the wage freeze and international liquidity. The Royal Shakespeare Company's pantomime *US*, is regarded as somehow relevant to the miseries of Vietnam. . . . Surely the theatre is the one thing in England that is treated seriously? It should not be so. In the old days actors were kept in place.

And eight years later when Ronald Reagan ran for president of the United States his former profession became the subject of jokes. There were no jokes about candidates who had been teachers, lawyers, or merchants before turning to politics.

Its roots being the psyche, prejudice against actors has reared its head in every civilization throughout history. It assumed the extreme form of an outright ban whenever puritanism triumphed, as in Geneva with Calvin, in England with Cromwell; it caused actors to be classed with the dregs of society, and to be persecuted by custom and law in the East and the West alike. In ancient Rome, actors were usually recruited from the ranks of slaves, while freedmen who entered the profession were classed under the law with deserters, panderers, habitual criminals. The *infamia* extended to their distant offspring; a third-generation descendant of an actor was not allowed to marry a third-generation descendant of a senator, lest he pollute noble Roman blood. In Imperial China, descendants of actors were not eligible for examination which opened the way to a career in public service. In France, as in other Christian countries, actors were not permitted to mingle with good Christians even after death; it took a revolution to give them the right to be buried in consecrated ground. In 1612, the British actor and dramatist Thomas Heywood published his celebrated *Apology for Actors* in which he tried with pathetic earnestness to prove that actors perform a useful function in society. Only two centuries later was this claim officially recognized when the greatest of them all, Henry Irving, was awarded a knighthood, at a time when almost every successful shopkeeper in England already had one (Queen Victoria was reported to have said on that occasion "we are very, very pleased").

Prejudice being motivated by causes hidden to the eye, it always seeks justification in rational arguments; we all know the specious, often self-contradicting arguments used to justify the persecution of minorities such as Jews, blacks, foreigners. The theatre and its practitioners have been attacked through the ages and frequently persecuted, on a variety of ostensible grounds.

The actor has been represented as immoral—especially in his sexual behavior—lazy, given to excessive drinking and other vices. In societies where hard work and thrift were considered supreme virtues, such as Europe in the beginning of the Industrial Revolution or America at the time of the Puritans, the actor was attacked for not engaging in honest work but "playing"—doing what children do: he still "plays" in English, *il joue* in French, *er spielt* in German, *hoo mesahek* in Hebrew—and for this he expects to be paid out of the earnings of those who actually work. And while acting is nowadays recognized as a legitimate pursuit, the popular image of the actor as someone who works only for a few short hours in the evening and spends his days loafing still persists. The general public is not aware, or refuses to be aware, of the long hours of rehearsals, of studying parts, of travelling.

Not only the actor but the theatre as such has been the object of a variety of accusations. It had been said that by showing such actions as murder, thievery, adultery, the theatre exercises a detrimental influence on the morals of the population. Puritans argued that by going to the theatre people wasted their money and time, both of which could be put to better use (a fairly valid argument in the days when the common people had little loose cash and even less leisure), that the theatre encouraged people to become spendthrifts by its display of luxurious attire and furnishing on the stage. Rousseau, in the previously quoted *Lettre sur les spectacles*, produced an original argument: since plays deal mostly with romance, and the latter is the natural domain of women, it tends to promote the social ascendancy of the weaker sex, which he considered detrimental to society. The prize for originality belongs, however, to a sixteenth-century Lord Mayor of London who came out against granting a license to build a new theatre on the grounds that "many hauing sores and not yet hart sicke take occasion hearby to walk abroad & to recreat themselves by hearing a play, whereby others are infected."[5]

In the West, the church was always in the forefront of all attacks against the theatre and against actors. Even before Tertullian, who in the second century forbade Christians to attend spectacles on pain of excommunication, church fathers spoke out against the theatre. Their argument was that the theatre reflected the pagan spirit of Rome with its displays of cruelty and obscenity. It was a sound argument, the Roman theatre of the time being the obscene monster that it was, but the attacks of the church continued in the centuries to come, regardless of the moral level of the theatrical art.

In 1694, when the French theatre was in its flowering, with the lofty works of Corneille and Racine performed by marvellously schooled actors, the church's most eloquent spokesman Bossuet published his *Maximes sur la comédie* in which he viciously attacked the theatre in general, the contemporary French theatre in particular, and saved his sharpest arrows for Molière.

The church sees in the theatre a competitor, because the theatre opens vistas to the audience that religion considers its exclusive domain. The power of the actor to lead the audience beyond the limits of everyday experience, to experiences of much greater intensity and purity, is a direct threat to organized religion. The church claims to be the sole possessor of this power.

"Religions based on transcendance, such as Islam, Catholicism, Protestantism, Jansenism," says the French sociologist of the theatre Jean Duvignaud, "have treated the actor with hostility, a hostility perfectly justified if one considers the real nature of the theatre and of the actor and of the imminent sources from which he draws. The sacred and the *mana* are locked in irreconcilable combat."[6]

There are even deeper reasons why Christianity, as well as Judaism, rejected the theatre. "God's world is a world of absolute, stable being" writes Jerusalem scholar Arieh Sachs, "a world of truth. The world of the jester is the world of the actor, lacking stability, assuming guises; in one word—a world of falsehood. The image of jesters in Jewish sources as men 'who do not recognize the truth . . . their very nature leaning to evil' contains an accusation similar to that of Plato's; the jester's sin is denial of the truth and of the divine order of creation, which is the only one deserving the concern of mortals.'"[7]

Among the laws the Lord gave to the children of Israel when they were still wandering in the desert was a prohibition of assuming guises, forbidding men and women the wearing of garments of the other sex, "Whosoever doeth these things is an abomination unto the Lord thy God" (Deut. 22:5).

The acting profession has always been associated in the public eye with sexual license, and has thus been regarded with a mixture of disapproval and envy. The image of the theatre as a breeding ground for free sexual practices was given additional ground in Europe in the second half of the sixteenth century when women took their place on the stage. In times when modesty was regarded as one of a woman's chief virtues, the home and hearth her sole province, it was naturally assumed, and much of the time with some degree of truth, that a woman who exhibits herself in public, be her attire as decorous as a nun's and may she confront her male partner at a distance only, was a woman of loose morals, and she was treated accordingly. In Italy during the *commedia dell'arte*, one of the theatre's great periods, it was not uncommon for an actress to have a stipulation in her contract to the effect that the company manager would receive a share of her profits from men. In Spain in the seventeenth century, during the so-called Golden Age, women won the legal right to appear on the stage, but were subjected to indignities when they did so. The playwright Juan Zabaleta left us a description of a Madrid young blood's manner of amusing himself at the theatre. Having gone to the theatre early, he wanders into the dressing rooms. "There he finds women taking off their street clothes and putting on their theatrical costumes. Some are so disrobed as though they were about to retire to bed. . . . The poor actress must suffer this and does not dare to protest, for, as her chief object is to win applause, she is afraid of offending anyone. A hiss, no matter how unjust, discredits her, since all believe that the judgment of him who accuses her is better than their own."[8]

The public image of the actress as a woman of loose morals has persisted through the nineteenth century despite the immense prestige enjoyed by such individual actresses as Sarah Bernhardt or Ellen Terry. It persists in our times of radically changed sex mores. Diana Rigg, England's foremost actress of the seventies, confided to a reporter how difficult it was to persuade her Yorkshire parents to let her go on the stage. To them, "being an actress was only one step up really from being a prostitute."[9]

The image also persists of the male actor as possessed of inordinate seductive powers. Irving Howe tells us in his *World of Our Fathers* how the Jewish immigrant community of New York at the turn of the century, a largely puritanical society based on tight family ties, delighted in the innumerable romances and trails of illegitimate children of the reigning monarch of the Yiddish theatre, Jacob Adler. "Theatrical royalty was granted special dispensation," the author concludes.[10]

And anyone who lived in the seventies anywhere in the world will remember how avidly the news media fed the global public with details of the intra- and extramarital affairs of members of movie royalty Elizabeth Taylor and Richard Burton. "Society looks upon the actor's tendency to deviate from norms with some sort of approval," writes the German sociologist Dieter Weidenfeld. "Society voluntarily relinquishes here social control, because society wants to keep the actor at a distance, not to consider him as a part of its cultural system."[11]

The actor is granted special privileges, writes Fenichel, due to his peculiar position in society. "The artist is still regarded as nearer to God, and enjoys the privileges of the priest. As is well known, the privileges accorded to the artist are very ambivalent in intent. The actor is privileged, but he remains somewhat beyond the pale of 'honest' society. He sins publicly and thereby exculpates the others (though he, subjectively, has the striving of being himself exculpated). Like the whore, he is held in contempt but envied."[12]

In *Totem and Taboo*, Freud mentions the custom prevalent among some primitive societies to build walls around "dangerous persons," such as chiefs and priests, to isolate them from ordinary members of the tribe; and he remarks that such walls still stand in modern society, royal protocol for instance. Early in time society built such a wall—constructed out of beliefs and customs, and even laws—around the dangerous person of the actor—a wall which over the centuries changed forms many times, but seems to be standing forever.[13]

NOTES

1. Quoted from Plutarch in A. M. Nagler, *A Source Book in Theatrical History* (New York: Dover, 1952), p. 3.

2. Jean-Jacques Rousseau, *Politics and the Arts: Letter to M. D'Alembert on the Theatre,* (*Lettre sur les spectacles*) trans. with notes and intro. by Allan Bloom (Glencoe, Ill.: Free Press, 1960), p. 79.

3. Otto Fenichel, "On Acting," *Psychoanalytic Quarterly* 15, no. 2 (1946).

4. David Belasco, *Acting as a Science*, quoted in *Actors on Acting*, ed. Toby Cole and Helen Krich Chinoy (New York: Crown, 1970), p. 582.

5. Nagler, *Theatrical History*, p. 116.

6. Jean Duvignaud, *L'Acteur: Esquisse d'une Sociologie du Comédien* (Paris: Editions Gallimard, 1965), p. 277.

7. Arieh Sachs, *Shkiyat Haletzan* (The Prankster's Decline), from proceedings of the Israel National Academy of Sciences (1978)5:28.

8. Juan Zabaleta, *An Afternoon at the Theatre*, quoted in *Actors on Acting*, ed. Cole and Chinoy, p. 73.

9. *Time*, 28 May 1979, p. 21.

10. Irving Howe, *The World of Our Fathers* (New York: Harcourt Brace Jovanovich, 1976), p. 476.

11. Dieter Weidenfeld, *Der Schauspieler in der Gesellschaft* (Cologne: Deutsche Artze Verlag GmbH, 1959), p. 37.

12. Fenichel, "On Acting."

13. Sigmund Freud, *Totem and Taboo*, in *The Basic Writings of Sigmund Freud*, trans. and ed. Abraham A. Brill (New York: Random House, Modern Library, 1938), p. 823.

1

The Glory That Was Greece, the Decline That Was Rome

> And so, when we have anointed
> him with myrrh, and set a garland
> of wool upon his head, we shall
> send him away to another city.
>
> Plato, *The Republic*

Nothing better illustrates the unique position of the tragic actor in Greek society than a remarkable document cut in stone and mounted in the theatre of Dionysos in Athens. It is a decree by the Council of the Greek Confederation spelling out all the privileges granted to Dionysian performers—actors appearing in festivals dedicated to that god.

The decree states, among others, that actors be given the security of person and property and exemption from arrest in time of war, that they be allowed to travel in the line of duty between countries at war, that they be exempt from military service; all this "in order that they may hold the appointed celebrations in honor of the gods at the proper season, and be released from other business, and consecrated to the service of the gods."[1]

This document clearly establishes the status of the actor as a priest. And it was as a priest that he appeared to the audience. Mounting the stage in the huge auditorium under the clear Mediterranean sky, literally larger than life, lifted as he was from the ground by the ten-inch *cothurnus*, the stiltlike boot, dressed in majestic robes, his face hidden behind a mask fashioned in a frozen expression of powerful emotion, his voice amplified by the mouthpiece in the mask and reverberating in the marvellous acoustics of the stone auditorium, the tragic actor recited some of the greatest poetry ever written, enacted events of tremendous magnitude, drawn from the depths of the collective memory of the people.

The place of the theatre in the life of ancient Greece demanded that the actor be of such stature. The theatrical performance was a national-religious event, part of the annual festivals to which Greeks travelled to the metropolis from their far-flung islands, the same as Jews journeying to the Temple in Jerusalem, the Moslems to Mecca.

The state made every effort to see that the largest number of citizens attend the performance. The indigent were given the two oboli which was the standard price of a ticket; women, who during that glorious period of cultural blossoming remained in domestic isolation, were encouraged to go to the amphitheatre; even slaves were allowed to attend, if they had their masters' permission. The Greek theatre, that is, theatre altogether, began when Thespis arrived in Athens from Icaria with his startling invention: the use of one performer to keep up a dialogue with the chorus, instead of the chorus merely reciting the poetry as was the practice until then. Little as we know about it, it seems that the Greek classical theatre to a degree remained true to its origin: recitation. There was no realistic acting, as we know it now, no scenery and no props, and hardly any of what we now call stage business. Wearing a mask with a set expression, making little use of his body, the *cothurni* and the heavy clothing severly limiting the performer's freedom of movement, the actor relied mainly on one instrument—his magnificently trained voice.

There is also good reason to believe that the Greek tragic actor did not strive to express the character of the person he portrayed, not as we understand it today. Male actors playing female roles—there were no women on the Greek tragic stage—did not even attempt to speak in female voices. The accent was on the poetry, its music and its inner meaning. Imitation, that is, externals, was limited to what would today appear as a most inadequate minimum.

Hidden behind the mask, the Greek actor did not offer his person to the public the way a contemporary actor does. He was not one man of flesh and blood imitating another. Lacking a face, he was an abstraction. What the viewer saw was the image created by the playwright, not the actor impersonating that image.

Given their popularity and high status, tragic actors occasionally attained exalted positions at court, and since their profession demanded that they travel from state to state, sometimes even crossing enemy lines, they were often entrusted with diplomatic missions. The actor Thetallus, a great favorite of Alexander the Great who loved the theatre with a passion, is known to have arranged the king's marriage with the daughter of a Carian satrap. So highly did Alexander think of Thetallus that when in 332 B.C. the actor lost a contest in Tyre, the mighty king dissolved in tears and told his courtiers that rather than seeing his favorite defeated he would prefer to lose part of his kingdom, though he did not specify which one.

Fame often went to actors' heads. Aristoteles, to whom we owe much of what is known on the Greek classical theatre and who was not above waspish gossip, reported that one Theodorus always insisted on being the first actor to mount the stage, on the questionable theory that this assured him the maximum attention. He would therefore take on even small parts if this only meant that he would be the first one to appear. As the importance of actors grew, at the expense of dramatists, stars allowed themselves to take liberties with the texts, tailoring parts to their own likings. Toward the end of the fourth century things had reached such a pass that Lycurgus, the Athenian minister of the treasury who financed the festivals, decreed that original copies of plays be placed in state archives to make it possible to check such abuses and punish the guilty. The actor Lycon, another favorite of Alexander, was fined the huge sum of ten talents for inserting lines of his own into a play—not that this much mattered to him since Alexander paid the fine.

At the time of the theatre's flowering, the importance of the actor reached its peak. Aristoteles wrote that actors were much more important than dramatists. It was generally assumed that the dramatist depended upon the protagonist, the chief actor, to win him the prize for the best play so he could become a national hero, his name cut in stone for posterity. Thus dramatists made every effort to secure the best actors for their plays. And as competition began to run wild, the management of festivals introduced a system of equitable distribution of prime acting talent. At the Lenaia festival in 418 B.C., Lysikrates and Kallipides, the two greatest actors of the period, acted in both competing tragedies. And in 341 B.C., at the Dionysian festival, the three competing dramatists Astydamas, Euaretos, and Aphareus, had the three greatest actors, Thetallus, Neoptolemus, and Athendores, appear in each of their plays, all this to ensure fairness, allowing the jury to judge each play on its true merits.

The theatre being a place of religious observance, its precincts were sacrosanct, as were the persons of the actors and of the poets whose works they performed. The audience was expected to behave with decorum appropriate to a sacred place; there is at least one known case of an Athenian citizen actually sentenced to death for forgetting himself to the point where he hit a man in a quarrel over a seat. He conveniently died of natural causes before the date set for the execution.

Curiously enough, all this did not prevent the audience from expressing disapproval of an actor's performance. Given the Mediterranean temperament, this disapproval was apt to take drastic forms. Not only were spectators hissing and shouting when the recitation did not sound true to their ears and the gestures were too extravagant, but they would pelt the performer with the figs and olives they brought along to refresh themselves with during the long hours of the performance, and even with stones which they must have carried just for this purpose, assuming that there were no loose stones lying around the amphitheatre. The legendary orator Demosthenes tells about his political opponent Aeschines, a former actor, who was forced to flee the amphitheatre with spectators in hot pursuit throwing stones after he gave a poor performance in *Thysestes*. There are even reports that spectators demanded on occasion that an actor be publicly flogged, and the "staff bearers," a special amphitheatre police, would oblige the audience on the spot.

If this kind of behavior appears shocking to us, especially in view of the religious character of the festivals, we must remember that since the festivals honored Dionysos, the god of wine, a great deal was being consumed by the crowds, spirits ran high, inhibitions were loosened. Greek comedy is full of references to the crop of illegitimate babies born nine months after the festival.

Aeschines, the actor who was nearly stoned, was a mere tritagonist, the third in the hierarchy of actors following the protagonist and deuteragonist, as Demosthenes pointed out, adding that not only was Aeschines a mere tritagonist, but a poor one too. We never heard of a protagonist being given such treatment, whether this was due to his superior talent or whether his position would prevent it.

To be a protagonist meant not only glory but large earnings as well. Most actors were fairly well paid. They were organized in guilds which protected their interests. In addition, the state saw to it that they should not be exploited by unscrupulous managers; the latter had to be licensed, and were required to take oaths to fulfill their contractual obligations toward the actors they hired for the festivals. Despite this, we find indications that run-of-the-mill actors did not fare well. Some led precarious, disorderly lives, and were accordingly held in low esteem. We know that there were indigents among actors: the guilds operated a welfare system to help those out of work; among others they maintained a house in Athens where actors returning from a tour with empty pockets could stay until something else turned up.

It can be assumed that those indigents were mainly mimes who had none of the status of tragic actors, and it was probably they to whom Aristoteles referred in a cryptic remark which speaks of actors' "general depravity," attributing this to the fact that they had to work for a living, as well as to their "habitual intemperance."[2]

The mimes, and to some degree the comedy actors, differed from their august colleagues, the tragic actors, by the fact that their art was based mainly on imitation, on taking on the character of another person and imitating events from daily life. The tragic actors were removed from daily reality both by the nature of the art, which was primarily the interpretation of poetry, and by the subject matter of the plays in which they appeared—events of such magnitude, so far removed from ordinary life, that they were barely real.

The distinction between the mime and the tragic actor is clearly voiced by Plato. In *The Republic*, Socrates discusses the matter with his friend Adeimantes who had just come back from the theatre. Having some doubts whether theatre should altogether be admitted to the Ideal State, Socrates is ready to make concessions for a "mode of narration such as we have illustrated out of Homer, that is to say, this style will be both imitative and narrative; but there will be very little of the former, and a great deal of the latter."[3]

Like Solon before him and like many religious and secular thinkers in centuries to come, Plato expresses through the mouth of Socrates his distrust of those who will stand up in front of an audience and imitate, impersonate. Evidently speaking of mimes, Socrates voices utter contempt for

> the sort of character who will narrate anything, and the worse he is, the more unscrupulous he will be; nothing will be too bad for him; and he will be ready to imitate anything, not as a joke, but in right good earnest, and before a large company. . . . He will attempt to represent the roll of thunder, the noise of wind and hail, or the creaking of wheels, and pulleys, and the various sounds of flutes, pipes, trumpets, and all sorts of instruments; he will bark like a dog, bleat like a sheep, or crow like a cock; his entire art will consist of imitation of voice and gesture, and there will be little narration.[4]

Then, in probably the best articulated and most explicit expression of the ambivalence with which society has always regarded the actor's art and his person, Socrates adds:

> And therefore when any of those pantomimic gentlemen, who are so clever that they can imitate anything, comes to us and makes a proposal to exhibit himself and his poetry, we will fall down and worship him as a sweet and holy and wonderful being; but we must also inform him that in our State such as he are not permitted to exist; the law will not allow them. And so when we have anointed him with myrrh, and set a garland of wool upon his head, we shall send him away to another city."[5]

A wide gulf separated the tragic actor from the comedian and the mime. Compare the first in his majestic robes, his face a mask of noble emotion, his body lifted from the ground by the *cothurnus*, with the comedy actor in his everyday dress or in rags, with padded front and aft which made him appear comically deformed, a huge phallus dragging on the ground or in full erection reaching up to his chest, playing the part of a ridiculous old man, a cunning slave, speaking bawdy lines to the delighted shrieks of the crowd. Or compare the tragic actor with the mime, a marvellously talented and trained performer, who, as Socrates said, could imitate anything. While the comedy actor's estate was well below that of the tragic actor, the estate of the mime hit social bottom; he was accorded the treatment reserved for mountebanks, street acrobats, and jugglers, from whom he was often indistinguishable. A Roman wall painting shows a duo of Dorian Greek mimes in action: one is performing on a rough platform, while the other is passing around the hat. We also have a detailed description of a performance of mimes in a wealthy Athenian home, from the pen of the historian Xenophon, a performance given to a distinguished audience which included Socrates himself.

The mimes were a boy and a girl, both the property of a Syracusan dancing master—the boy also doubling as the master's concubine, as the Syracusan casually informed those present. The two enacted in words, gesture, and dance the romance of Dionysos and Ariadne, the girl demonstrating her talents as actress, dancer, and acrobat. We can assume that the two little slaves belonged to the upper reaches of the profession, performing as they did in those distinguished surroundings.

The gulf separating tragic actors from comedians and comedians from mines narrowed almost to the vanishing point when the Greek theatre was transplanted to Rome. There, everybody appearing on the stage was marked with infamy, and it did not matter whether the stage was built of marble in a lavishly endowed amphitheatre, or was made of planks hastily nailed together on a market place. In Rome, unlike in the land of its birth, the theatre was not part of a national-religious observance. The actors were mere entertainers, their sole task was to please the crowds. As such they were subject to all the prejudices attached to their profession. And to make their position in Roman society even worse, most of the early performers were Greek slaves of freedmen, and were as such considered not entirely human in the Roman scheme of things.

Historian Cornelius Nepos ruefully compared the situation in his country with that which had prevailed in Greece: "Even to appear on the stage and exhibit oneself to the people was never regarded as shameful by those nations. With us, however, all those acts are classed as either disgraceful or as low and unworthy of respectable conduct."[6]

Cicero, a lover of the theatre and a friend of actors, testifies that "since they [the Romans] considered the dramatic art and the theatre in general disgraceful, they desired that all persons connected with such things should not only be deprived of the privileges of other citizens, but should even be removed from their tribes by sentence of the censors."[7]

Cicero's use of the third person may imply that he dissociated himself from the prejudices of his compatriots. This is not true, however. Elsewhere, in another context, he says in passing that he found it incongruous that a man of such fine character as his great friend Roscius should be an actor.

The prevailing attitude toward actors was made into law. The Code of Justinian states flatly that "he who appears on the stage in order to act in shows is marked with infamy." *Infamia* was a legal term which meant that a person so marked was deprived of the various civic and personal rights to which Roman citizens were entitled. It thus placed actors in the same category as convicted thieves, panderers, and soldiers dismissed from the service in disgrace. The law also made invalid marriages contracted by actors or their offspring with descendants of persons of senatorial rank.

The actors' social status was naturally reflected in the manner in which they were treated by their employers. In the epilogue to Plautus's comedy *The Casket*, the narrator bids farewell to the audience, and announces that those actors who made no mistakes in the performance will get drinks, while those who did will be flogged.

Public flogging was common punishment meted out to actors for the slightest offences, with government officials given the right to order it at their own recognition. The distinguished actor Hylas was once flogged in the atrium of his house for an unspecified misdeed, as was Pylades, a famous mime who had the audacity to point a finger at a member of the audience who hissed at him. Following the flogging, Pylades was banished from Italy, which meant a virtual end to his career.

A similar fate befell the comedian Stephanio who was banished after being flogged on three consecutive evenings in three different theatres—a punishment personally ordered by Caesar Augustus. The emperor's ire was aroused when he learned that a lady of senatorial rank, who disguised herself as a boy, was found waiting for the actor at the stage entrance. We do not know what happened to the lady.

By so severely punishing an actor for alleged sexual misconduct, the emperor gave expression to the common belief that actors were endowed with extraordinary seductive powers. This belief was also expressed in the law: a man had the right to kill an actor on the spot whom he found in *flagrante delicto* with his wife.

On the bottom of the social ladder of the profession were, of course, the mimes, a motley crowd ranging from performers of rare accomplishment to low-grade mountebanks. It can be assumed that their moral conduct was not of the highest, in keeping with the mode of life to which they were relegated and with the nature of the performances they gave. At its worst, a mime show was frankly obscene. It was the only kind of show in which women were allowed to appear, and they appeared wearing only a short, loose garment which exposed more than it concealed, and which they often removed to the "take it off!" shouts of the audience.

So wanton were the performances of mimes that Aelius, a contemporary writer, speaks of the behavior of a low whore as being as indecent as that of an actress in mime. One of those actresses, a beautiful woman who, according to an eyewitness, the historian Procopius, "outshamed the most shameless dancers," entered history as Empress Theodora, the wife of Emperor Justinian of Byzantium.

Adultery was one of the most frequent subjects of mime shows, and given the Romans' penchant for realism, scenes of adultery were shown in every realistic detail. Emperor Heliogabalus, a great mime fan, is reputed to have given orders that the audience be thus given its money's worth. Realism also reigned in other areas; we have at least one recorded case of an execution actually performed on the stage. The reluctant actor was Lauredus, a convicted murderer; the audience saw him die on the cross as part of a scheduled show.

Mimes were performers of many skills; at their best they were exquisitely sophisticated, capable of telling a most complicated story by means of gesture alone, with the accompaniment of music and sometimes with a narrator added. Lucian of Samosata, a second-century admirer of the mime's art, related how the great Paris, a famous mime of the period, made a convert of the philosopher Demetrius who had spoken disparagingly about mimes.

Paris responded by inviting Demetrius to a performance in which he appeared all by himself with no assistance of musicians, singers, or narrator.

> He was as good as his word. The time beaters, the flutes, even the chorus, were ordered to preserve a strict silence; and the pantomime, left to his own resources, represented the loves of Ares and Aphrodite, the embarrassment of Ares, his entreaties—in fact the whole story. Demetrius was ravished at the spectacle; nor could there be higher praise than that with which he rewarded the performer. "Man," he shrieked at the top of his voice, "this is not seeing, but hearing and seeing, both: 'tis as if your hands were tongues!"[8]

Despised as a class, placed outside the law, mimes were the pets of high society. The historian Pliny the Younger tells the story of Ummidia Quadratilla, an eighty-year-old lady of high rank and great wealth who owned a troupe of male mimes and enjoyed their performances both at her parties and in the privacy of her bedchamber. The lady's grandson, a young man of high moral principles, would leave the house when Ummidia considerately informed him that a performance was to take place.

Ummidia Quadratilla was no exception. During the first and second centuries A.D. it was customary for every grand house to keep a resident troupe of mimes. The owners would occasionally hire them out to impresarios and collect the fee. Good mimes were considered a profitable investment; they earned large sums for their masters. Naturally, the Imperial household had its pick. Mnester, one of the great mimes of the period, was the property as well as the lover of Caligula; he was also the lover of Empress Messalina for which both eventually paid with their heads.

For a while Paris was a resident at the court of Nero as a close friend and boon companion to the emperor. However, royal favor, being notoriously fickle, he was eventually beheaded; a would-be actor himself, Nero could not suffer someone more talented near him for any length of time.

It was during the reign of Nero that the popularity of mimes in high society reached its peak. The law forbidding senators and knights to seek their company was totally ineffective, flouted as it was by all, including the Imperial family. Empress Domitia led the way by taking as a lover a mime also named Paris, to which the emperor Domitian responded by beheading the actor. The tragic death of the mime plunged Roman society into mourning. For weeks processions of ladies of rank visited the spot where the precious blood was spilled, pouring fragrant oils and strewing flowers on the ground. Martial, the gossipy chronicler of the time to whom we owe much of our knowledge of the manners and morals of the Imperial Rome, was moved to write this heartrending epitaph: "Wanderer on the Via Flaminia, do not pass this noble marble monument. The delight of Rome, the wit of Alexandria, art, grace, merriment, joy, the glory and grief of the Roman stage, and all the goddesses and gods of love lie here buried with Paris."[9]

As popular as the mime shows and often indistinguishable from them were the *Atellanae*, a native coarse comedy which had its origin in rural amateur shows. It was customary there to spike the dialogue with topical references, which required of the actors a sharp and quick wit. It also required a great deal of daring, for though *Atellanae* actors were given the court jester's license to say publicly what was forbidden to others—even to criticise the sacrosanct person of the Emperor—they paid dearly when they did not know where to stop. Nero banished from Italy an actor who delighted the audience with a reference to the generally known fact that the emperor had poisoned his father and drowned his mother. The comedy in which the actor appeared had a line "oh father, oh mother"; when pronouncing it, the actor made gestures simulating drinking and swimming. Another actor fared much worse. When he allowed himself a joke about Caligula, the emperor lived up to his reputation by having the culprit burned alive in the stadium.

Tragic actors in Rome never achieved the fabulous popularity enjoyed by stars of the lesser theatrical arts. One great name has been preserved for posterity, that of the second-century tragedian Aesop, a Greek who started out in life as a slave, and retired at a fairly young age to enjoy his wealth and eminence. No longer a practicing actor, he became free, to a degree, of the stigma attached to his profession.

One reason why Greek tragedy did not strike deep roots when it was transplanted into the soil of Rome was the fact that in the second century tragedy was no longer the lofty, pure art of Sophocles and Euripides; and removed from its origins, it deteriorated further. Lucian of Samosata, who so admired the art of the mime thus describes a tragic performance of his time:

> In forming our estimate of tragedy, let me consider its externals—the hideous, appalling spectacle that the actor presents. His high boots raise him up out of all proportion; his head is hidden under an enormous mask; his huge mouth gapes open upon the audience as if he would swallow them; to say nothing of the chest-pads and stomach-pads with which he contrives to give himself an artificial corpulence, lest his deficiency in this respect should emphasize his disproportionate height. And in the middle of it all is the actor, shouting away, now high now low—chanting his iambics as often as not; could anything be more revolting than this sing-song recitation of tragic woes? The actor is a mouthpiece; that is his sole responsibility; the poet has seen to the rest, ages since.[10]

No wonder then that when the inhabitants of a town in Baetica first saw a performance of a tragedy they ran in panic from the amphitheatre. At the very most, tragedy was accepted only by the educated minority, while efforts to bring the masses to the amphitheatre were largely unsuccessful. Those efforts were very elaborate indeed. Catering to the Roman masses' love of spectacle, the impresarios embellished their shows with elaborate sets and costumes, adding such extra attractions as marching troops, chariots, ships, war booty, white elephants in full panoply, lions, giraffes. Cicero, a man of refined taste, once walked out in disgust on such a performance.

Greek comedy fared slightly better in the favor of the masses, and reached a peak with the popularity of the incomparable Roscius whose name was to become the synonym of perfection. Born into the peasant class, of an unprepossessing appearance aggravated by a squint (he was the first comedian to wear a mask, supposedly to hide this handicap), Roscius was the epitome of studied elegance, admired by the crowds, imitated by generations of actors. He was showered with money and favors, the first and only actor in Rome to be elevated to knighthood—a distinction which in Rome also carried considerable monetary rewards—by his friend and protector, the dictator Sulla who was as fond of rewarding his favorites as he was of beheading those who displeased him.

Roscius's greatness and his fabulous career were immortalized in a speech by Cicero, his close friend and legal counsel as well as his pupil in the art of oratory. The speech was delivered in court where Cicero pleaded for his client in a litigation brought by one, Fannius. The latter had given Roscius co-ownership of a slave named Panurgus. When Roscius trained the man to become a successful comedian who commanded large fees, Fannius wanted the deal cancelled. Cicero argued that Panurgus, the actor whose co-ownership Roscius acquired for next to nothing, was wholly a creation of his teacher, and his prominence was mainly a reflection of his master's glory. "What hopes, what expectations, what enthusiasm, what favor accompanied Panurgus on the stage, because he was the pupil of Roscius. All who were devoted to Roscius and admired and favored and approved of the pupil; in short, all who had heard the name Roscius thought Panurgus an accomplished and finished comedian."[11]

Roscius marks the height of achievement of the Roman theatre. After him the curve points downward. Spectacles were becoming bigger and bigger and theatre buildings were becoming more and more magnificent, as the emperors spent more and more lavishly to please the restless masses; and the art of theatre was drowning in all that opulence, with obscenity and cruelty becoming increasingly prominent as the people's taste coarsened. The lines separating tragedy, comedy, and mime became blurred, as did the lines between actors and gladiators, men who killed and had themselves killed for pay. The importance of spectacles in the life of the people in both Rome and the Eastern Empire increased to a ludicrous size as festival followed festival. In the year 345 A.D. there were 175 festival days with stage performances. In the fifth century, when barbarians from the north repeatedly sacked the city, destroying many public buildings, the first ones to be rebuilt were the theatres. The barbarians despised the Roman theatre for its immorality, but when the Ostrogoth king Theodoric ruled Rome in the beginning of the sixth century, he had to keep on financing spectacles or face a massive revolt. So did his successors. By then the spectacles were hated with a passion by the Christian church, already a major power. The end came in Rome in the year 568, following the Lombard invasions; in the Eastern Empire spectacles continued for another century. In 682 the Synodus Quinisexta of the church issued a ban on all spectacles. Thus, in the melancholy words of theatre historian Karl Mantzius, "ancient dramatic art ended its existence with a hideous, lascivious grimace."[12]

As the long night descended on Europe, the theatre ceased existing. The tradition was kept barely alive in the pathetic performances of strolling mimes, jugglers, acrobats, and tellers of heroic and ribald stories to ignorant listeners, who wandered from village to village, occasionally invited into castles, persecuted by the church, loved and despised by the people. The tiny flicker in the darkness did not burst into a flame again until about six centuries later.

NOTES

1. Karl Mantzius, *A History of Theatrical Art in Ancient and Modern Times*, vol. 1, trans. Louise von Cossel (New York: Peter Smith, 1937), p. 177.

2. Aristotle, *Problems*, quoted in Sir Arthur Pickard-Cambridge, *The Dramatic Festivals of Athens* (London: Oxford University Press, 1933), pp. 131-32.

3. Plato, *The Republic*, trans. Benjamin Jowette, quoted in *Actors on Acting*, ed. Toby Cole and Helen Krich Chinoy (New York: Crown, 1970), p. 10.

4. Ibid.

5. Ibid., pp. 10-11.

6. Cornelius Nepos, *Praefatio* (Cambridge: Harvard University Press, Loeb Classical Library, 1931).

7. Marcus Tullius Cicero, *De Republica* (Cambridge: Harvard University Press, Loeb Classical Library, 1931).

8. Lucian of Samosata, *Of Pantomine* in his *Dialogues* (Cambridge: Harvard University Press, Loeb Classical Library, 1931).

9. Ludwig Friedlander, *Roman Life and Manners under the Early Empire* (London: Routledge & Kegan Paul, 1965), p. 115.

10. Lucian, *Of Pantomine*.

11. Cicero, *Quintius Roscius Comedian* in his *Speeches* (Cambridge: Harvard University Press, Loeb Classical Library, 1931), p. 301.

12. Mantzius, *History of Theatrical Art*, p. 238.

2

All Spectacles Are
Celebrations of the Devil

We thank you, Almighty God,
for making our place in the
houses of worship and of study
and not in theatres and circuses.

> Rabbi Nehunia Ben Hakana
> (1st century)

Caesarius, Bishop of Arles in the beginning of the sixth century, one of the great preachers of the era, coined the pithy phrase that expressed the church's attitude toward the theatre. "Omnia spectacula pompae diaboli sunt," all spectacles are the celebrations of the devil, said Saint Caesarius in one of his famous sermons.[1]

The bishop's repeated attacks on the theatre are, of course, the best proof that spectacles were still being held in Arles in his day, and that they were attended by Christians. The town in the south of France was in those days an important commercial and political centre, and one can still see a fairly well-preserved Roman theatre there among other remnants of its former glory. Part of the stage is missing; it was removed by orders of Bishop Hilarius about fifty years before his successor Saint Caesarius preached his sermons. It was an act both symbolic and utilitarian, because the well-hewn stones were needed for a church the bishop was building.

The church's campaign against the theatre had started much earlier, at the very beginning of institutionalized Christianity, and it continued, in one form or another well into the nineteenth century. As late as 1860, Monseigneur Ignace Bourget of Montreal said *ex cathedra* that "even a small taste of the theatre is enough to condemn a believer."[2]

The list of church fathers who denounced the theatre and inveighed against the immorality of actors on and off stage reads like a who is who among the saints, and includes such names as Saint Augustin, Saint Jerome, Saint John Chrysostomos, and Saint Cyprian. Hardly a church council passed without the matter being dealt with, until the year 692 when the Synodus Quinisexta delivered the coup de grâce: following the council's decision, Emperor Justinian II issued the final ban on spectacles.

The first of the church fathers to speak out against spectacles was Tatian, a second-century missionary and prolific writer, an ascetic who opposed all pleasures of the flesh including the eating of meat and the drinking of wine, and eventually sex even within the bonds of marriage. He was closely followed by Tertullian, the most eloquent of the Christian foes of the theatre, a militant theologian and proselytizer. His *De Spectaculis*, a treatise on the evils of the theatre, remained for centuries the basic Christian text on the subject.

Tertullian tells there about a Christian lady who had gone to see a show. Punishment was swift: an evil spirit entered her body. When the exorcists came, the spirit argued: "I had the right to enter her body because I found her on my own ground."[3]

The theatre was in Tertullian's eyes an impure place that polluted everyone who entered. "You will fatigue by applauding an actor those very hands which you have raised towards the Lord," he cried out. He knew a great deal about spectacles and their technical aspects, evidently the result of frequenting the theatre before his conversion. He was also well acquainted with the history of the theatre, using its pagan origin as a powerful argument. Living at a time when spectacles were so much a part of the life of the people in the Empire, when the state spent huge amounts of money in the amphitheatres to keep the restless masses happy, when mimes were idolized and showered with favors by the upper classes, Tertullian was well aware of Roman society's ambivalent attitude toward actors. "Men surrender their souls and women their bodies as well, while at the same time keep them excluded from all privileges of citizenship," he declared. "On one and the same account they glorify them and they degrade and diminish them. What perversity! They love whom they lower; they despise whom they applaud; the art they glorify, the artist they disgrace."[4]

Though he was well informed on the theatre in all its aspects, Tertullian made no distinction between tragedy and mime shows, and even gladiatorial contests, in order to emphasize the immoral character of spectacles. Here is an obviously prejudiced description of a show:

> Its supreme charm is above all contrived by its filth—filth in the gestures of the actor of the farce—filth acted by a buffoon playing a woman, banishing all sense of sex and shame, so that they blush more readily at home than on the stage—filth that the mime undergoes, in his own person, from boyhood, to make him an artist. The very prostitutes, the victims of public lust, are produced on the stage, more unhappy in the presence of other women—the only class in the community whose notice they escape; they are paraded before the faces of every rank and age; proclamation is made of their abode, their price, their record, even before those who do not need the detail; yes, and more (and I say nothing of the rest) that ought to be hidden in the darkness of their dens and not pollute the daylight. Let the Senate blush; let all ranks together blush. Those women themselves, who have murdered their own shame, shudder (you can see it in their gestures) to find themselves in the light and before the populace, and blush once a year."[5]

One can easily understand the revulsion of an early Christian, with all the puritanism inherent in his faith, to the kind of a show he describes. Some students of the subject maintain that the church's antagonism to spectacles was not an integral part of the teachings of Christianity, and that the church fathers did not oppose spectacles as such, only spectacles of the revolting kind that prevailed in the Roman Empire of their times.

The French scholar Moses Barras calls our attention to the fact that though council after council denounced the theatre, no such condemnation ever came from an ecumenical council or from the Pope. He also notes that Saint Augustine publicly confessed that he enjoyed shows, and that Saint Thomas outrightly defended shows and the acting profession. "Amusements are necessary for the preservation of human life," wrote Saint Thomas. "Among things useful for this end, one may count some licit professions, such as that of actors, which tend to give solace to men. This profession is not illicit in itself and actors are not in a state of sin provided they act with moderation, that is to say, without illicit acts or words, and that they refrain from acting in circumstances and at times when it would be out of place."[6]

Saint Thomas was an exception; the spokesmen for Christianity in the later centuries followed Tatian and Tertullian. As late as the eighteenth century, the celebrated Bossuet, a French theologian and preacher of formidable authority, wrote a book against the theatre in which he repeated the arguments of the church fathers, though the French theatre of his days was imbued with Christian spirit and was a model of moral purity. Moses Barras himself sadly admits that Saint Thomas's defense of the theatre "although it embarrassed theologians considerably . . . was not accepted for many centuries."[7]

When we consider the church fathers' attitude toward spectacles, we must also remember that Christians in the immediate past had been reluctant performers, in such casts as included lions. In a less spectacular form of intolerance, the Roman stage also was used frequently to ridicule and malign Christians. Incidentally, one such comedy supplied the church with a saint, later adopted by Catholic actors as their patron. Genesius, an actor who flourished in the beginning of the fourth century, in the reign of Diokletian—the last of the great persecutors of Christianity—was appearing in a comedy in the role of a man about to die. As the doctors despaired of his life, he cried out that he wanted to die a Christian, a priest was brought in to perform a mock baptism complete with all sort of obscenities to delight the crowd. At a performance graced by the presence of the emperor, Genesius rose from his deathbed and, addressing himself to Diokletian, declared: "This is not a show, I really am a Christian." Needless to say, he was punished by death.[8]

Though the main burden of the Christian argument was the immorality of the stage and its pagan spirit, the church fathers did not ignore the fundamental issue, namely that there is no room in the Christian world for two kinds of priests: one officiating at the altar, the other on the stage. Tertullian exulted:

What a spectacle is already at hand, the return of the Lord now no object of doubt! What exultation will that be of angels, what glory that of saints as they rise again! What the reign of the righteous thereafter! What a city, the new Jerusalem! The theatre on earth, on the other hand, is based on a lie and therefore opposed to religion. The Author of Truth loves no falsehood, all that is feigned is adultery in his eyes. One who changes his voice, sex or age . . . will not win God's approval, because God condemns hypocrisy."⁹

The attacks on the theatre gained in intensity when Christianity came out from underground eventually to become the state religion. The early Christians were so possessed of religious fervor that they did not need spectacles for spiritual nourishment, but the masses that accepted Christianity out of convenience or under pressure were ordinary citizens who liked their entertainment the same as anyone else. This forced the church to take such extreme measures as excommunicating theatre goers long after actors had been placed beyond the pale. When proselytes were baptized, they had to renounce spectacles, and a lapse caused automatic excommunication. It was a relentless war carried out with all the formidable weapons at the church's disposal, a war that lasted centuries, as long as the church exercised power in the state. Only the French Revolution led to the abolition of laws that prevented actors from exercising the rights of citizenship, and not until 1849 were actors in France officially recognized as Christians in good standing. Cruel laws prevailed against actors wherever the Catholic church exercised power; in 1779, a prominent Polish actress gained the posthumous distinction of being the first of her calling to be buried in consecrated ground, and this only because she was the king's favorite and he personally intervened. Not that Protestants had any greatly different ideas on the subject. It was thanks to Cromwell that England had no theatre in the seventeenth century, it was Calvin who banned the theatre in Geneva in the sixteenth, and it was the Protestant clergy in the United States in the beginning of the nineteenth century who led the battle against early American theatre.

The antitheatre literature produced by men of the church is voluminous and rich, and some of it makes very good reading. A number of church fathers display admirable erudition in the matter, evidently the result of frequenting shows before they saw the light, and some of their descriptions read more like advertisements than condemnation. We learn from them about the free and easy mingling of the sexes in the theatre, of the displays of women's charms on the stage, of explicit sex scenes. Quoting some of those graphic accounts, Moses Barras, a French scholar writing in rather unsure English, remarks that the church fathers feared "especially the effect of actresses upon the male members of the audience."[10]

The most eloquent foe of spectacles was the fiery orator Saint John Chrysostom (Mouth of Gold). One of his sermons is worth quoting:

> What tumult! What satanic clamor! What diabolic dress! Here comes a youth, with hair combed back which makes him effeminate in look and manner, in dress, aye, in everything takes on the shape and guise of a tender girl. Here comes an old man with hair all shaved, who cast off shame with his hair, and who stands there to receive slaps on the face and who is prepared for all that is said and done. And the women too! With uncovered heads, all shame lost, they stand talking to people, aiming at unchastity, arousing the minds of spectators to wantonness and obscenity. For those wanton words, those ridiculous manners, those foolish tonsures, those ways of walking, those dresses, those voices, that softness of limb, that winking of eyes, those pipes and flutes, those dramas and arguments—aye, all are full of wantonness. Here are to be seen naught but fornication, adultery, courtesan women, men pretending to be women, and soft-limbed boys.[11]

One can better understand Saint John Chrysostom's anger if one considers the popularity mime shows enjoyed among the faithful, including senior clergy. It was during that period that Pope Eusebius saw fit to issue a warning to bishops not to have at their dinner parties "histriones, buffones, acrobats," which was a widespread practice among the ecclesiastical as well as secular nobility of the fifth century. So popular were such spectacles among the prelates that when a wealthy Alexandrian lady named Peristea left in her will a large sum of money for cloisters, Bishop Dioscoros who was entrusted with the bequest "expended the money on actresses and other theatrical persons," as a contemporary chronicler notes in a rather ambiguous phrase. The same chronicler informs us that Dioscoros's brother, the bishop of Ephesus, not only attended shows, but would go to the theatre dressed as Dionysos.[12]

For the student of theatrical history, the obsessive hatred of spectacles by men of the church is a blessing in disguise. It is largely due to them that we know something about the theatre in the Dark Ages, for hardly any other records exist. Out of that obviously prejudiced source emerges a melancholy picture. Allardyce Nicoll, the eminent authority on the subject, waxes sadly poetic when describing the state of the theatre, if the spectacles seen in those days could be called theatre at all.

> The airy lightness of a classical city is metamorphosed into the twisting alleys of a medieval town. The world which once listened to a gracious Greek and a precise Latin has its ears filled with the guttural notes of a Germanic victor or the base accents of a provincial priest. Christianity has conquered, and the age of gold, the age of silver, has become the dark age—dark in thought and dark in record. The mimes are singing and jesting as Rome falls; were they able to keep their songs and their merriment alive during the time when Europe was in convulsion, when all serious men thought only of eternal salvation?[13]

The question is a rhetorical one. There were mimes and jesters and minstrels and *jongleurs* and *minnesingers* and *spielleute*, entertainers given various names by various peoples, roaming Europe, east and west. According to Edmund K. Chambers,

> They wandered at their will from castle to castle, and in time from borough to borough, sure of their ready welcome alike in the village tavern, the guildhall, and the baron's keep. They sang and jested in the market places, stopping cunningly at a critical moment in the performance to gather their harvest of small coin from the bystanders. In the great castles, while lords and ladies supped or sat around the fire, it was theirs to while away a long bookless evening with the courtly *geste* or witty sally. At wedding or betrothal, baptism or knight-dubbing, treaty or tournament, their presence was indispensable.[14]

Those favorites of the common folk and of lords were outcasts living on the margins of society, outside the ecclesiastical law which was the law of the land, refused whatever rights a citizen enjoyed in those dismal days, deprived of the services of the priesthood which was the only solace to which men could then turn.

According to Chambers, the life of a minstrel meant "To tramp long miles in wind and rain, to stand wet to the skin and hungry and footsore, making the slow bourgeois laugh while the heart was bitter within; such must have been the daily fate of many amongst the humbler minstrels at least. And at the end to die like a dog in a ditch, under the ban of the Church and with the prospect of eternal damnation before the soul."[15]

The clergy would not rest. Council after council repeated the condemnation; in 1183, in Chalon-sur-Saône, it was decided to punish ecclesiastics who attended shows by suspending them from office. Earlier, upon request of the clergy, Charlemagne promulgated a law edifying all the previously prevailing restrictions concerning spectacles. One item is of special interest: it provides for corporal punishment of actors who perform in ecclesiastical garb. This would tend to indicate that some of the shows mocked the clergy.

One lonely, daring voice rings out of all that shrill, hostile clamor. Choricius of Gaza, a sixth-century Greek philosopher, moralist, art critic, and rhetorician, wrote an *Apology for Actors* in opposition to the clergy's contention that all frivolity is bad. On the contrary, Choricius argued, laughter is good since "man is distinguished from the brute by this god given quality." Countering the most frequently used argument that shows are evil because they often portray evil actions, he pointed out that men of such high moral stature as Homer and Aeschylus portrayed evil deeds. Choricius asked,

> Of what indeed can the mimes be accused, unless you charge them with the crime of not imitating the better only? And how could they be worthy of the word "mime", which is theirs because of the portrayal of life, if they were to delineate some parts of life and neglect others? . . . Instead of blaming the mimes, blame those who commit the evil actions which are themselves the basis of the miming, or imitation of evil. When we thus reflect on the matter we see that the actors are not guilty of any crime.[16]

Did any of the despised mimes rise to fame and fortune as did their colleagues in other, happier times? A luckily preserved epitaph tells of one. His name was Vitalis, and he lived probably in the ninth century, somewhere in western Europe. The epitaph, written in the first person, extolls both the glory and the skills of the artist. "Here in this town I won fame; here a rich house I had; and here applause was showered on me, for I made people glad." Among his many skills was female impersonation, as we learn from the following: "When I spoke I so changed my face, my habit so altered, and tone, men thought that many were there where I stood alone. How oft did they laugh to see, as I mimicked a dainty wife, my gestures so womanly quaint, the shy blush done to the life!"[17]

There were mimes in eastern Europe, moving up from Byzantium to Russia. We hear about *skomorokh*s, "wandering legend-tellers who disseminated all over the country different plays and songs about events connected with 'the great time of troubles,' about Ivashka Bolotnikov, about battles, victories, and the death of Stepan Riazin," [Russian folk heroes].[18]

As in the West, the Russian wandering performers were held in low esteem, and met with the enmity of the Orthodox church. Under the latter's pressure, laws were enacted to limit the performers' activities. Probably in order to justify the treatment they were accorded, a contemporary chronicler wrote that the *skomorokh*s wandered "in bands of sixty, seventy, and even a hundred men, forcibly taking food and drink from the Christians in the villages, abducting animals out of their stables, and causing bodily injuries to people on the roads."[19]

It seems that mimes were very well established in England in the thirteenth century, as we learn from an eminent ecclesiastic, Thomas de Chabham, Bishop of Salisbury. A foe of the mimes, as becoming his position, the bishop was objective enough to make a distinction between "good" and "bad" *histriones*, as he called them. "There are those who change the shape and appearance of their bodies, gesticulate and leap in a disgraceful manner, wear monstrous masks or even appear in the nude; there are those who are attached to the retinue of a lord and entertain dinner guests with singing, or tell stories glorifying the deeds of noble knights and Christian martyrs." The latter were, of course, the good ones; not only because of the subjects they treated, but because they practiced simple singing and narration without indulging in sinful imitation.[20]

While militating against the mimes, the church realized that the mimetic instinct of the people could not be suppressed, and therefore should be turned to the church's advantage instead. Thus the liturgical and later mystery and morality plays came into being, which attempted to accomplish—in an infinitely cruder fashion—what the ancient Greek theatre did: present in a vivid form and in the vernacular the mythology and moral values of Christianity. It was a theatre aiming at the edification of the faithful who no longer understood the Latin of the prayers.

The spectacles began rather modestly in the church, with the priests and their acolytes as the performers. As they eventually moved out of those confines into the streets and town squares, the cast was joined by laymen and the spectacles became bigger and more ambitious, with elaborate costumes and large, complex sets and machinery needed for the representation of the death and resurrection of Christ, the lives and martyrdom of saints, the sufferings of evildoers in hell, the Last Judgment. The church theatre eventually became so elaborate that it rivaled the huge shows of Imperial Rome, lasting days, even weeks, with the entire town involved in the preparations and performances.

Since the spectacles served religious purposes, and since the performers were amateurs who received no pay, though they often invested much time in rehearsals, no stigma was attached to their appearance on the stage. On the contrary, participation in a mystery play conferred upon a citizen great distinction and enhanced his position in the community.

In *The Life and Sufferings of Saint Barbara*, a fifteenth-century chronicle, we read about a barber's apprentice named Lyonard of Metz who was so successful in his portrayal of Saint Barbara, the heroine of the play, that all noblemen in the area offered to adopt him. The lad who was evidently as clever as he was talented, accepted instead the offer of a canon to provide for his education, and he was sent to study in Paris where he became a canon himself. In the same city of Metz, a girl of common origin who acted the role of Saint Catherine, did even better by marrying a rich nobleman.

The prestige attached to appearing in a religious play was not diminished by the fact that some of the amateurs had to play roles of villians, such as Herod and even the Devil. What they did have to suffer was some physical discomforts. The *chaldeans*, Russian peasants performing in the traditional "furnace show," a Christmas feature enacting the story of Daniel, had the worst of it: at the conclusion of the show they had to take a dip in the river—in the Russian winter—in order to cleanse themselves after wearing pagan clothes.

Even frontal nudity, to use a modern term, was allowed in the name of religion. In a passion play written by one Grabens, the High Priest orders the executioner to strip Jesus before nailing him to the cross, so that he should be "as naked as an earth worm, and neither for prayers nor entreaties must you allow him to keep, at the top or at the bottom, large, middling or small pieces of garment with which to hide one single spot." In order to make quite sure that he heard him right, the man asks the High Priest "You want him as he came out of his mother's womb?" and the answer is "Exactly." And evidently afraid that this exchange was not explicit enough, the author added the stage direction: "Here they strip Him quite naked."[21]

The spectacles reached a peak of splendor by the end of the fifteenth century but the seed of decay was already present. As the Middle Ages waned, and with it the religious fervor of the people and the power of the church, secular and frivolous elements infiltrated the religious plays, and side by side with ordinary citizens professional actors began to appear. The veil of darkness was lifting, the theatre was ready for a triumphant return.

NOTES

1. Quoted in Juergens Heiko, *Pompa Diaboli* (Berlin: Verlag Hohlammer, 1972), p. 204.

2. Jean-Claude Germain, "Théâtre Quebeçois or Theatre Protestant?" *Canadian Theatre Review* (Summer 1976), p. 10.

3. Tertullian, *Di Spectaculis* (Loeb Classical Library, 1931), p. 291.

4. Ibid., p. 285.

5. Ibid., p. 275.

6. G. Larroumet, "Revue de G. Mangras, *Les Comédiens hors la loi*," *Revue Politique et Littéraire*, 22 October 1887, p. 517.

7. Moses Barras, *The Stage Controversy in France from Corneille to Rousseau* (New York: Phaeton, 1973), p. 20.

8. Heinz Kinderman, *Theatregeschichte Europas*, vol. 1 (Salzburg: O. Müller, 1957), p. 208.

9. Tertullian, *Di Spectaculis*, p. 297.

10. Barras, *Stage Controversy in France*, p. 20.

11. Quoted in Allardyce Nicoll, *Masks, Mimes, and Miracles* (London: Harrap & Co., 1930), p. 138.

12. Ibid., p. 137.

13. Ibid., p. 135.

14. Edmund K. Chambers, *The Medieval Stage*, vol. 1 (London: Oxford University Press, 1903), p. 44.

15. Ibid., p. 48.

16. Nicoll, *Masks, Mimes, and Miracles*, p. 142.

17. Toby Cole and Helen Krich Chinoy, eds., *Actors on Acting* (New York: Crown, 1970), p. 37.

18. B. V. Varneke, *History of the Russian Theater* (New York: Haefner Press, 1971), p. 7.

19. Ibid., pp. 7-8.

20. Karl Mantzius, *A History of Theatrical Art in Ancient and Modern Times*, vol. 1, trans. Louise von Cossel (New York: Peter Smith, 1937).

21. Ibid.

3

The Great Awakening

I'll come no more behind your scenes,
David; for the silk stockings and
white bosoms of your actresses excite
my amorous propensities.

Samuel Johnson

The darkness began to lift toward the end of the fifteenth century and as the new century dawned, there was a bright light sweeping Italy, soon to spread throughout all of Europe. While the wealthy and the educated were delighting in the rediscovery of the classical past, and scholars and clergymen were giving recitations of noble Latin verse in ducal palaces, the common folk found equal delight in the comedies and farces performed by lowly strolling players who were about to develop one of the greatest theatres the Western world has known, the commedia dell'arte.

Strangely enough, it was the Italian clergy which led the way in the revival of the classical theatre, the princes of the church staging performances in their palaces of a splendor to rival those of the secular magnates. The church's traditional enmity toward the theatre was suspended, as were other traditions of the church in those years of grace, especially since the performances were dignified by being in Latin, the language of religion and scholarship and, moreover, were unsullied by the appearance of unprofessional actors. The performers were all amateurs, clergymen and scholars. One prelate did not limit himself to the role of impresario, but also wrote his own plays.

Cardinal Bibiena was the author of the immensely popular *Calandria*, a comedy based on Plautus's *Menaechmi*, which the cardinal spiced up with bawdy scenes out of Boccaccio. *Calandria* enjoyed a vogue lasting several decades; it was performed at most ducal courts in Italy and, given the hosts' virtually unlimited financial resources, the performances were of extraordinary splendor. The world première took place in 1513, at the court of the Duke of Urbino. One of the directors of the production, Baldassare Castiglione, described the show in a letter to a friend:

> The Stage represented a very beautiful city, with streets, palaces, churches, and towers. The streets looked as if they were real, and everything was done in relief, and made even more striking through the art of painting and well-conceived perspective. Among other things there was an octagonal temple in low relief, so well finished that it seems hardly possible that it could have been built in four months even if one considers all the potential workmanship which the state or Urbino can master.[1]

Theatricals became a status symbol among the wealthy and powerful. On the occasion of the wedding of his son, the Duke of Mantua gave a performance in his private theatre which seated a mere five thousand spectators. Five comedies, all in Latin, were presented to the captive audience, each of the comedies enlivened by interludes of music, ballet, and spectacles demonstrating the immense ingenuity of the Duke's stage engineers. In one memorable scene, hundreds of girls, gorgeously attired as angels, floated under the ceiling, the scenes intended as homage to the innocence and purity of the bride, Lucrezia of the house of Borgia. The splendor of production made up for the woefully poor acting by amateurs whose sole qualification was the ability to recite Latin.

In sharp contrast to those performers were the actors of commedia dell'arte, the professionals, a motley crowd of ragged semi-literates who spoke only lowly Italian dialects and performed on improvised stages of rough planks. The men and women, the latter surreptitiously or openly eking out their meagre earnings by entertaining men off stage, were beggarly characters who "lived from hand to mouth practicing their art under many vexatious restrictions from church and state, taxed for the benefit of the poor, the clergy and the prince, and unable to regulate their affairs save in the narrowest limits."[2]

The commedia dell'arte was an actor's theatre par excellence, more so than any theatre ever known: the actors disposed with the services of a playwright, or rather reduced him to the role of a scenario writer, fleshing out his skeletal plot with improvised dialogue and stage business; tricks which could rise to the heights of feats of acrobatics and sleight of hand such as chasing an imaginary fly around the stage or, for no apparent reason, make a few somersaults without spilling a drop of water from a glass in hand. Needless to say, they had to be quick thinkers, always ready with a repartee or a flow of grandiloquent prose. At their best, they were probably the most highly skilled actors in the history of the Western theatre.

Nicolo Barbieri, or Beltrame as he was known on the stage, was one of the leading commedia dell'arte actors, as well as an author of scenarios. He also wrote *La Supplica*, one of the many "apologies" actors have written over the ages to justify their profession.

Making a distinction between "respectable" and "disrespectable" actors, Barbieri objected to comedians being referred to as buffoons, the latter being, in his opinion, low entertainers with limited skills who produce a laugh with "an ugly grimace, a headlong tumble, a monkey-like gesture, imitating a little puppy or cat." Comedians, on the other hand,

> study and fortify their memory with a wide variety of things such as sayings, phrases, love speeches, reprimands, cries of despair, and ravings, in order to have them ready for the proper occasion. Their studies are suited to the character of the person they portray; and since more actors play serious parts than ridiculous ones, they devote themselves more to the study of serious matters than to gay matters. Hence, the majority of them spend more time studying how to make audiences cry rather than laugh. For laughter can be created more easily by an exaggerated word or gesture than by a studied and carefully presented one; but it is a difficult thing to make an audience weep at things that everyone knows not to be true.[3]

As often happens to apologists of oppressed groups, Beltrame accepted all the prejudices to which his profession was subject, in order to stress the superiority of actors of his kind:

> The buffoon is one who has no virtue in him but who, nimble and impudent by nature, seeks to live for good or ill by his wits; or if he possesses some little virtue, he exploits it for buffoonery, making the audience hoot at even serious persons by pointing out annoying defects in them. A buffoon is one who stands with his hat on his head in front of his prince; who says insulting things to gentlemen; who assails honor in sharp-tongued phrases; who tells dishonest tales; who for money sometimes allows his entire head to be shaved; who indulges in furtive tricks; who filches whole wax candles; who eats vile foods; who gambles furiously and behaves cowardly because of his greed for money. A gentleman, however, who has some virtue and is by nature gay and gracious, is never a buffoon, but a lively spirit, dear to princes, respected by knights and desired by women.[4]

In the words of Winifred Smith, those actors "worked to create a beautifully expressive art, to diffuse the culture of their country abroad and to add to it at home; all together suffered opprobrium and honor, lavish reward and unjust punishment; all strove more or less unconsciously, more or less successfully, to better their social position, to put the actor's career on a par with the poet's and painter's, and to bring the professional actor class into a better repute than during the middle ages the church had allowed it to hold."[5]

One of the most significant aspects of the commedia dell'arte was the employment of women on the stage, instead of having men play female parts as was the custom, as well as the law, until then. This both raised the standards of performance, and gave a new argument to the foes of the acting profession. Actresses became identified in the public eye with prostitution, as they had been in the distant past when they appeared in mime shows. Beltrame was well aware of this reputation of his female colleagues. He wrote:

> Somebody will object. I have courted an actress, and it did not take much time to gain my end with her. But all women are not equally ready, and all men are not equally successful. There are men

who pursue a woman for years, and sacrifice treasures for her sake, without obtaining anything but a dismissal. And besides, actresses are women like others, and nature has not favored them with the privilege of resisting love more than others. They cannot err without it being known by all, and, religion apart, they are bound to be more careful and discreet in their behavior than the women who can cover their fault with the cloak of hypocrisy.[6]

Some actresses did, in fact, lead exemplary private lives. The most famous of those was Isabella Andreini, considered the greatest actress of her time and genre, and one of the great actresses of all times—if we are to accept the extravagant praises lavished on her by contemporaries.

Isabella Andreini was too good to be true. A woman of stately beauty, she was not only an actress but an accomplished singer and dancer. She was a prolific poetess and dramatist, and a woman of learning at a time when learning among women, even in the highest social circles, was rare. She was a friend of the mighty and the learned, a famous wit who could hold her own with the greatest conversationalists of her time, as at that famous dinner given in her honor by a cardinal, where the guest list included six other cardinals and the poet Torquado Tasso, a writer whose correspondence with the great intellects of her time was posthumously published in six volumes.

Isabella Andreini's private life matched her other accomplishments. Married at an early age to Francesco Andreini (the leading man of the famed Gelosi company, which she joined at the age of sixteen); she remained married to him for twenty-six years until her death at forty-two, while pregnant with her eighth child. Of the seven children she left, all four daughters took the vows, one son became a priest, another took up professional arms, and one followed in his parents' footsteps to become a distinguished actor and scenario writer. Upon Isabella's death, Francesco Andreini vowed never again to appear on the stage and eventually entered a monastery.

Her death occurred in Lyons where she was then appearing. The city gave her a magnificent funeral, and she was buried in a church. Francesco affixed over her grave a bronze plate with an epitaph commemorating "a woman pre-eminent for virtue, the ornament of morality, faithful to her marital relations, religious, pious, a friend of the Muses, the chief of theatrical artists, who here await her resurrection."[7]

Isabella Andreini was, of course, an exception, one of the precious few who gained a social position of note, mainly thanks to the good graces of the nobles whom they served. Most of the companies, or "academies" as they called themselves for no particular reason, were maintained by noble houses, which made them subject to the caprices of their powerful sponsors. A number of attempts were made to organize independent companies, but none of them lasted. In all those attempts stress was laid on outward respectability. One academy included in its statute the requirement that each member go to confession at least three times a year, and that a member who hears another one swear must denounce him to the Inquisition.

Obviously, those rules were meant to placate the local clergy which, the bishops and cardinals notwithstanding, made life difficult for the wandering troupes. In 1568, the Bologne clergy issued a statement listing a number of reasons why comedies should not be allowed. The arguments were standard: "They play for the most part lascivious and dishonest pieces which corrupt good morals"; the actors are "generally vagabonds of ill repute, who carry about with them women of bad life"; their performances are attended by "courtesans, young men and boys, whence arise occasions for a thousand sins." While not demanding that performances be banned altogether, the padres ordered a number of restrictions. Among others, the actors were forbidden to appear on the stage in clerical garb, which would indicate that some of their shows mocked the priesthood.[8]

Companies enjoying high patronage were free of restrictions, as long as they remained in the patrons' favor, which was notoriously fickle. Even the Gelosi with their international fame, with the two Andreinis in the lead, had their ups and downs, and ended up sadly, exiled by their patron, the Duke of Mantua, from his domain.

The incident throws a curious light on the relations between princely patrons of the arts and artists of that era. It seems that the duke was very amused by a play the Gelosi performed, a comedy in which all characters were hunchbacks. After the performance, he summoned the actors and asked who was the author of the piece. Two of them claimed the distinction, each hoping for a generous gift from the ducal purse. Irritated by their quarrel, the duke summarily ordered them both beheaded. They were eventually pardoned, but not before they were put to torture and were expelled from Mantua together with the rest of the Gelosi.

As for the glorious Andreini family, nine years after Isabella's death, her son Giovanni Battista, a celebrated actor and scenarist in his own right, wrote to his former patron a letter of unbelievable self-degradation, begging for a handout, recalling the services rendered by his parents and himself to the house of Mantua. The letter closed with the following words: "I make my reverance to you, and also to your most Serene Mother, whom I humbly petition for the favor I am begging, that is the concession without delay of the merest justice to me, and so, kneeling to you both, I kiss your garment."[9]

The Italian acting troupes travelled far and wide, to Spain, France and even England where, the language barrier notwithstanding, they enjoyed great popularity, and left their mark on the theatre of those countries. In Spain, the country closest geographically and linguistically, their influence was the earliest and the strongest. The Golden Age of the Spanish theatre owes a heavy debt to the Italian commedia dell'arte.

Not that Spain in the period of the Renaissance did not have any blossomings of its own. There was the *auto sacramental*, a religious play that grew out of church services whose purpose was to imbue the populace with the sense of importance of the sacraments, performed in conjunction with the Corpus Christi festivals. There were also beginnings of a secular theatre starting around 1500. They centered around the person of Lope de Rueda, considered the first *autor de comedias*, an actor-manager who also wrote the plays for his company. He was well acquainted with the Italian theatre, and his plays showed its influence but he drew his themes and characters from Spanish folklore.

A few of his performances, given in the Valladolid city square, were attended by a twelve-year-old boy named Miguel de Cervantes.

About fifty years later the author of *Don Quixote* recalled the experience.

> In the time of the celebrated Spaniard [Lope de Rueda], all the properties of a theatrical manager were contained in a sack, and consisted of four white pelices trimmed with gilded leather, and four beards and wigs, with four staffs, more or less. The plays were colloquies or eclogues between two or three shepherds and shepherdesses. The furnishings of the stage were an old woolen blanket drawn by two cords from one side to another, which formed what is called a dressing room behind which were the musicians, singing some old ballad without the accompaniment of a guitar.[10]

A much more detailed and entertaining description of life in the Spanish theatre of the period can be found in *Entertaining Journey*, a novel by Augustin de Rojas, a sixteenth-century writer, actor, and adventurer. One chapter of the novel finds the actor-hero and his companion down and out on the road. Things look utterly bleak when they meet a travelling company, and are asked to join them.

> We led this happy life for more than two weeks, eating little, traveling much, with the theatrical baggage on our backs, and without ever making the acquaintance of a bed. Going in this way from one village to another, it happened to rain a good deal one night, so, on the next day the director told us—and it was only a short league to where we were going—to make a litter of our hands and carry his wife, while he and the other two men would carry the baggage of the company, the boy taking the drum and the other odds and ends. The woman being quite satisfied we made a litter with our hands, and she wearing a beard [a mask meant to protect her complexion from bad weather] we began our journey. In this way we reached our destination, completely worn out, foot-sore and covered with mud; indeed, we were half dead, for we were serving as pack mules.[11]

Women were allowed in those days in Spain to appear on the stage, as they were in Italy. A ban issued by the king under the pressure of the church was short-lived and never really enforced while it lasted. When the ban was formally abolished, a proviso was added that only actresses whose husbands or fathers were employed by the company were allowed to appear. The edict also included the curious proviso that no gentleman was to visit an actress more than twice.

Though protected by husband or father, the actress was in no enviable position; she was fair game to Spanish dandies who thought nothing of going backstage to watch her dress for a performance, and generally behaved in the presence of actresses in an offensive manner.

The playwright Juan Zabaleta wrote with great bitterness about the manner in which actors were treated by the public. Describing a particularly ugly incident caused at the theatre by a Madrid idler, he asked:

> Why do they do this? . . . Besides being foolish and cowardly to treat them thus, it is most ungrateful, for of all people actors are those who strive hardest to please. The rehearsals for a *comedia* are so frequent and so long that it is often a positive torment. And when the time for the first performance arrives, every one of them would willingly give a year's pay to make a good appearance on that day. And when they come on the stage, what fatigue, what loss would they not willingly undergo to acquit themselves well of their task? If they cast themselves from a rock they do it in the fearlessness of despair, yet their bodies are human, and they feel pain like any other.[12]

Life was difficult even without being treated this way by the public. In his *Entertaining Journey*, de Rojas occasionally drops the bantering tone to give vent to his bitterness:

> There is no . . . slave in Algeria but has a better life than the actor. A slave works all day, but he sleeps at night; he has only one or two masters to please, and when he does what he is commanded, he fulfills his duty. But actors are up at dawn and write and study from five o'clock till nine, and from nine till twelve they are constantly rehearsing. They dine and then go to the *comedia*; leave the theatre at 7, and when they want rest they are called by the President of the Council, or the *alcaldes*, whom they must serve whenever it pleases them. I wonder how it is possible for them to study all their lives and be constantly on the road, for there is no labor that can equal theirs.[13]

The theatre also suffered from frequent bans. In 1646, all playhouses were closed for about five years, the ban caused by "disorder and looseness" in costumes and performances. Theatres were also closed following a death in the royal family, forcing actors to look for employment elsewhere. In 1611, after the death of the dowager queen, Lope de Vega wrote a letter to a powerful nobleman asking his intervention to save actors from death by starvation.

Yet the profession flourished. A remarkable document entitled *Genealogía, origen y noticias de los comediantes de España*, compiled between the years 1700 and 1721, lists thousands of actors. We learn from the source that some of the actresses, contrary to the reputation of their calling, were ladies of signal value; a certain Maria de Riquelme was so virtuous that forty years after her death her body was found in a state of perfect preservation, a privilege usually reserved for saints. Another one whom the *Genealogía* says lived "evangelically" eventually left the stage to enter a convent, as did many other actresses of her time. On the other hand, one actress murdered her actor-husband with the complicity of a lover, a mere prompter, as the chronicle contemptuously notes. She was sentenced to death, but thanks to the intervention of her uncle, the great comedian Juan Raña, was given a royal pardon, and went on with her career so successfully that she eventually became an *autora*, a company manager.

The general tone of the *Genealogía*, which was probably compiled by one or more actors, is apologetic, an attempt to prove that actors, their profession notwithstanding, were like other people. There were among them, we learn, even persons of "noble lineage," such as the great *autor* Alonso de Olmedo y Tofino. The *Genealogía* quotes a royal decree which says that despite his having engaged in a profession unbecoming a gentlemen, he and his children were not to be disqualified from holding public office.[14]

France awoke to the theatre considerably later. The reasons were chiefly political: only in the beginning of the seventeenth century did the country emerge from a civil war which had lasted almost half a century, and life returned to normality. Paris moved toward becoming the cultural centre of the country—and of the Western world. Progress was unbelievably rapid, as if the theatre was determined to make up for time lost. About sixty years after the French theatre began to awake from its medieval slumber it outdistanced the rest of Europe to reach a height unequalled by any other country.

Before it all started, France had its *bateleurs* who replaced the jongleurs and histriones, roving bands of entertainers living from hand to mouth, appearing at fairs and other public gatherings. They were persecuted by the secular authorities and the church alike, were often banned in various localities, the most frequently advanced argument being that they made people spend money which rightfully belonged to the poorbox in church. Lowly as those performances must have been, they were of some quality; we know that Molière as a young man enjoyed them, and he later admitted that he learned a great deal from them.

Some of those entertainers achieved considerable celebrity. There was the great Tabarin who set up a medicine show with his wife and brother on the Pont Neuf in the heart of Paris, entertained there the multitudes, and sold quack medicines. This practice earned him the enmity of both the actors who sold tickets to their performances—seeing unfair competition in his free shows—and, of course, of the medical profession. There were also complaints from the ladies on Ile de la Cité whose maids, sent to do the shopping, forgot to come back.

So popular was Tabarin with the Paris populace that one day, when a rumor spread that he was going to dye his famous hat black, traffic around Pont Neuf was blocked for hours. Legend has it that Tabarin eventually retired to an estate near Paris to lead the life of a country gentleman. His well-born neighbors found it demeaning to have a former mounteback living in their midst, and staged a hunting incident in which he was shot dead.

The bateleurs, as well as the Italian troupes visiting Paris, had to overcome the opposition of the Confrérie de la Passion, an organization originally founded to present amateur religious theatricals and held a government-granted monopoly on public shows. They had branched out to comedies and farces, and occasionally employed professional actors who accepted their offers reluctantly because the pay was low and uncertain. The Confrérie, which had the support of both the secular and the ecclesiastical authorities, was so powerful that in 1543 they induced the Paris Parlement to forbid performances of bateleurs altogether under pain of flogging and banishment.

In 1548 the Confrérie erected its own building, the Hôtel de Bourgogne which was destined to play an important role in the history of the French theatre. In the same year the church authorities banned the Confrérie's religious plays because they had long been getting out of hand. However, the organization by then had become so firmly entrenched in its commercial interests that it was granted a monopoly on secular performances in Paris; thus no theatrical performances could be given in the capital outside the Hôtel de Bourgogne where the Confrérie acted as impersarios and collected commissions.

We know about the conditions under which actors worked in those days from a number of fortunately preserved contracts. In one of them, the actress Marie Fairet, the wife of the town crier, agreed with Antoine l'Esperonnier, "player of histories, to help him to play during the time indicated as much and as often as he chooses in the art of playing ancient pieces of Rome, consisting of several moral histories, farces and soubressaux." For those services she was to receive the sum of twelve *livres* a year, a sum by no means lavish, but constituting only part of her earnings. The pretty Marie, married or not, expected also to receive gifts of clothes and money from admirers. The contract stipulates that "Gailharde, wife of said l'Esperonnier was to receive one half thereof."[15]

They were nearly all rascals, wrote Tallement des Reaux, a contemporary gossip, in his *Histoiriettes*, "and their women lived in great licentiousness; they were used by the whole company, even by actors who were in different troupes." When a young man who served as secretary to Richelieu was indiscreet enough to invite an actress friend to a performance of a play in the cardinal's palace, he had to atone by making a public statement declaring that actresses were all strumpets.

Nothing is more illustrative of the low esteem in which the acting profession was held in France of the early seventeenth century than the story of Mathieu Le Fèbvre, known by his stage name Laporte. When he and his wife, both leading actors of the period, retired from the stage to spend the rest of their lives as respectable citizens in the town Sens, Laporte applied for and received a "letter of rehabilitation" from Louis XIII. In this letter the king stated that the actor came of good family but was incited in his youth by unworthy persons to join the theatre which, in his youthful naiveté, he considered a praiseworthy profession. Having realized at a mature age that the profession was not approved by serious people, he decided to retire, and live a blameless life from then on.

Contemporary chronicles mention many individuals who led decent lives despite being actors. We read of one actress, a "very beautiful creature of a woman who, contrary to all ordinary rules of the profession, was refined in manners and conversation, and any-one who had not known about it would not have believed that she was an actress. Several young men of Bordeaux fell in love with her, so much for her gentle and refined conversation as for her beauty." As a young girl she fell in love with an actor, an unscru-pulous man, who in his "debauched attitude" forced her to go on the stage. When the man died, she retired, and spent the rest of her life "correctly and honorably."[16]

A certain Bruscambille, a "prologuist" at the Hôtel de Bour-gogne and, as his writings would indicate, a fairly well educated man, felt compelled to write an "apology" for the acting profes-sion, as had the Italian Barbieri a century earlier. He, too, aimed chiefly at dissociating himself and actors like him from the lower reaches of the trade, the buffoons and bateleurs who toured the provinces, performed in the streets, and sold quack medicines. One was not to confuse those lowly creatures with "comédiens," Bruscambille insisted, with actors who "represent by their action the pure and true microcosm of nature's comedy," respectable, serious artists in whom some people see "libertines, vagabonds, useless to the public and marked by every type of infamy." The ancient Greeks honored such men as Thespis, and "Roscius walked on the level of the greatest noblemen of Rome." As for the atmo-sphere prevailing in the theatre, Bruscambille found it superior to that of the gambling house, the tavern, the brothel; a young man can find in those places "an infinity of debaucheries one hundred times more perilous than the theatre, and more expensive."[17]

Bruscambille's apology notwithstanding, prevailing prejudices were not without foundation in fact. We read in contemporary reports that some of the farces performed in his Hôtel de Bourgogne were exceedingly crude and foulmouthed; lines given to women were so obscene that it was hard to find actresses sufficiently shameless to utter them in public, so men had to play the parts. An actor named Alizon became famous for his portrayals of foulmouthed old harridans.

There were a number of companies, however, that tried to live up to the standards set by Bruscambille. One of those was founded by a young man named Jean Baptiste Poquelin. The son of a prosperous upholsterer, a *valet tapissier* to the king, young Jean disregarded the wishes of his father who wanted him either to join him in the business or move up the social ladder by studying law, and he entered instead the profession which in Bruscambille's phrase offered a life "sans souci et sans six sous." An energetic organizer, he put together a fine company and obtained the patronage of the Duc d'Orléans, which entitled the players to call themselves *Troupe de Monsieur*. They presented mainly tragedies in the grand manner and, according to reports of witnesses, did it rather badly.

Poquelin, who eventually assumed the stage name de Molière, had enough sense to give up tragedy and turn to comedy. In the triple role of manager, playwright, and actor, he created the greatest comedy the world has ever known—and, incidentally, made comedy more socially acceptable, attracting a better audience, and securing the patronage of Louis XVI. A consummate actor himself, he also attracted and developed first-class talent, among them stars like Michel Baron, Madeleine Bejart, and her sister Armande, who eventually became Madame Molière.

The prestige of the company and royal patronage did not prevent the young bloods of Paris from behaving in Molière's theatre as they would in a brothel. In a little court entertainment entitled *Les Fâcheux* (The Impertinents), Molière has a character identified as the Marquis thus describe the behavior of a Parisian gallant:

> I was got upon the Stage in a Humor hearkening to the Piece, which I had heard cr'd up by several persons: the Actors began, and every body was silent, when with a blustering Air and full of Extravagance, in brushes a Man with huge Pantaloons, crying out Soho there! A Chair quickly! and surpris'd the Audience with his great Noise! being interrupted in one of the most beautiful Passages of the Piece.[18]

Molière could afford to criticize his social betters publicly because of his position, the fame and recognition he enjoyed, and the favor of the king which expressed itself in lavish gifts of money and privileges. Royal power, however, stopped at the doors of the church. Stricken after a performance of *Le Malade Imaginaire*, Molière sent for a priest, but none came, even though the dying man sent word that he was ready to renounce his profession and declare that he had sinned all his life by appearing on the stage. He died without receiving sacraments, and the bishop of Paris refused to have him buried in consecrated ground. At the plea of the widow the king intervened, and the bishop agreed to compromise: the deceased was to be buried in the cemetery, but in an unmarked grave, after sunset, with only two priests present. To this day, the exact place of burial is unknown, and doubt remains whether he was actually buried in the cemetery proper, or in a portion of the cemetery reserved for those undeserving of Christian burial.

The church's enmity toward France's greatest playwright did not end with his death. Twenty-one years later, in 1694, the celebrated theologian and preacher Bossuet published his *Maximes sur la comédie*, one of the most violent attacks on the theatre ever written, and Molière was singled out as the chief offender.

NOTES

1. Quoted in A. M. Nagler, *A Source Book in Theatrical History* (New York: Dover, 1952), p. 71.

2. Quoted in Winifred Smith, *Italian Actors of the Renaissance* (New York: Coward McCann, 1930), p. 5.

3. Nicolo Barbieri, *La Supplica*, quoted in Toby Cole and Helen Krich Chinoy, eds., *Actors on Acting* (New York: Crown, 1970), p. 3.

4. Ibid., p. 54.

5. Smith, *Italian Actors of the Renaissance*, p. 14.

6. Ibid.

7. Ibid., p. 53.

8. Ibid., pp. 26-27.

9. Ibid., p. 183.

10. Cervantes, Preface to *Ocho Comedias, Comedias y Ocho Entre- meses Nuevos*, quoted in Hugo Albert Rennert, *The Spanish Stage of the Times of Lope de Vega* (New York: Hispanic Society of America, 1909), pp. 17-18.

11. Augustin de Rojas, *Viaje Entretenida*, quoted in Rennert, *Spanish Stage*, p. 169.

12. Juan de Zabaleta, *Día de Fiesta por la Tarde*, quoted in Rennert, *Spanish Stage*, p. 336.

13. de Rojas, *Viaje Entretenida*, p. 159.

14. N. D. Shergold, *A History of the Spanish Theatre* (London: Oxford University Press, Clarendon Press, 1967), pp. 532-33.

15. Rosamond Gilder, *Enter the Actress: The First Woman in the Theatre* (New York: Theatre Arts Books, 1959), p. 87.

16. W. L. Wiley, *The Early Public Theatre in France* (Cambridge: Harvard University Press, 1909), pp. 87-88.

17. Ibid., p. 82.

18. Molière, *Les Fâcheux*, quoted in Nagler, *Theatrical History*, p. 193.

4

Between the Merry Elizabethans and the Dour Puritans

In deede I muste confess there comes
to playes of all sortes, old and young;
it is hard to say that all offend, yet
I promise you, I will swear for none.

Stephen Gossen, *Schools of Abuse*

The most glorious period in the history of the British stage lasted a little less than a century and can be neatly enclosed within two dates: Queen Elizabeth's accession to the throne in 1558, and the victory of the Puritans in 1642.

During that remarkable period the English theatre rose from its humble status of wandering "Players of Enterludes" to an art form of surpassing brilliance and depth, loved by both the humble and the mighty, its achievements culminating in the dramas of Jonson, Marlowe, Shakespeare, its actors rising from the estate of vagabonds and rogues to that of settled, fairly well rewarded professionals. All of which took place in the face of the relentless hostility of the Parliament, of the city of London, and other municipalities. The theatre was caught in a tug of war between the royal court and the nobility with their humanist ideals on one side, and the rising bourgeoisie motivated by the ideals of Puritan morality on the other. When in 1642 the Parliament decreed that "all Stage-Players, and Players of Enterludes, and common Players, are hereby declared to be, and are, and shall be taken to be Rogues, and punishable,"[1] it was only to translate a long-standing attitude into law. To the Puritans the theatre was an institution immoral by its very nature; its practitioners were engaging in an immoral, frivolous pursuit, living on money earned by others in honest labor.

The Elizabethan theatre grew out of two sources: there was the native popular theatre of medieval origin, feeding on historical and biblical plays, on tales of chivalry, performing low comedy for the masses; and, at a much later date, there were dramas inspired by the classical writers, composed and performed by scholars in the universities and inns of court.

There was probably little artistic merit in either of the two, the former with its ramshackle plays catering to an undemanding audience, the latter with its imitations of Plautus and Seneca performed by learned clerics and dons. But they provided the dry bones which came to life when touched by the breath of the spirit of the time. And the spirit of the time was magnificent, with England broadening both its physical and spiritual horizons, Sir Francis Drake and Sir Walter Raleigh roaming the far seas, Shakespeare marvelling at that wonderful creature which is man. A perfunctory examination of contemporary plays of the period will show the confluence of the two sources, resulting in a theatre which appealed to both the illiterate and the educated, the common people and the wellborn.

Still, even at the peak of the Elizabethan theatre's accomplishment and recognition, the odor of disrepute never left it. The public theatre, attended as it was by persons from all walks of life, had not become the kind of place to which a respectable citizen could go with his wife and friends to spend a civilized evening. Physically a ramshackle affair, the theatre was more often than not flanked by a bear-baiting ring and a "stew house." The "groundlings" were apprentices who sneaked out of their shops, soldiers on leave, sailors ashore, women of ill repute plying their trade. On the balconies were students, intellectuals, members of minor nobility. Persons of quality, fops, aristocratic idlers, paid for seats on the stage where they sat decked out in the ridiculous finery of the period, making loud remarks, carrying on conversations. The groundlings milled around, ate and drank, and would even start a friendly game of cards when things were slow on the stage. The actors had to work very hard to keep the audience's attention, even merely to be heard above the din.

When Elizabeth ascended the throne, there was not one single theatre building in London. In 1574, James Burbage—the father of Richard, the first great Shakespearean actor—built the first permanent theatre. In the next quarter of a century at least ten more were erected.

The establishment of permanent homes for theatrical companies was a giant step toward making the theatre respectable; it helped remove from the profession the stigma of vagabondage which had clung to it since the Middle Ages. Another step toward respectability was securing the patronage of the royal court and the noble houses. In the well-ordered, highly structured, postfeudal Elizabethan society each man was expected to have his set place, which to the majority of citizens meant having a master. "Who are they? Who is their master?" Hamlet asks about the strolling players. Acquisition of a master also offered a company protection from harassment by local officials, in addition to giving them a place in the social structure.

The maintenance of companies of players by noble houses was a complex matter. Originally the actors were servants whose function was to entertain their master and his guests; eventually the handfuls of entertainers grew into full-fledged theatrical companies which travelled throughout the country on a commercial basis when not needed at home. Some of those troupes became so well established on their own that the connection with their lord grew more and more tenuous until it became nominal only. And as time went on, independent companies which had become prosperous sought the patronage of a lord for legal purposes only. The livery and the badge of a noble house offered protection. It was a mutually profitable arrangement; even when he did not reap any financial benefit, a troupe travelling under his badge added lustre to the lord's house.

Some lords used their players for political purposes. During the turbulent era following Henry VIII's break with Rome, with England riven by religious strife, the theatre was often used to promote one side or another with plays especially written for the purpose. Queen Elizabeth put an end to that; religious plays were forbidden altogether, and a gentleman or nobleman who wanted to maintain a troupe had to obtain a license. Plays also had to be licensed by the Master of Revels, a Court official who earned huge sums of money. He was paid £2 for every play he licensed, then £3 a month for every running show, plus the revenue from two annual benefit performances given by each licensed theatre—altogether about £4,000 a year. The average annual income of an actor at that time was £60.

The earliest and most important of the companies was the Earl of Leicester's Men led by John Burbage. They performed all over England, but when their lord needed them he would summon the actors from wherever they were at the time to his court or to the royal court to entertain the queen. Eventually the relationship became nominal only, as the company rose to become London's leading public theatre.

Noble patronage was of vital importance in the companies' unending struggle for their very existence. In 1572, when a municipal order was issued in London against the "masterless men, not using any lawful merchandise, craft or mystery," such as "fencers, bearwards, common players in interludes and minstrels, not belonging to any Baron or honorable person of greater degree," the Earl of Leicester's Men applied to their lord for a stronger affirmation of their relationship. In their petition they begged him to "vouchsafe to retain us as your household servants and daily waiters."[2]

One must, of course, make allowances for the expressions "household servants" and "daily waiters" which have little of the connotations attached to them today. Also the craven tone of the letter sounds worse to our ears than it must have to the ears of contemporaries. What the letter shows is that dire need for a badge, literally so, of respectability and social usefulness.

The theatre in which the Earl of Leicester's Men were playing, the first one in London, was built on a yard adjoining the Red Lion Inn. This set a precedent; innkeepers began to build scaffoldings in their yards to house acting troupes. It was a natural, mutually profitable arrangement, as the inns provided a ready-made audience, and those who went to see shows also availed themselves of the opportunity to quench their thirst.

The companies flourished, and the city was making a handsome profit out of licensing fees and taxes. When the royal court wanted to cut in on the profits, requesting that the licensing be done by the queen's officials, the Lord Mayor vehemently refused, whereupon the court retaliated by issuing a Letter Patent to Leicester's Men, a history-making document which for the first time gave formal, legal recognition to the acting profession, and, by the way, gave Leicester's Men sort of a monopoly on theatre performances in London, entitling them to "use, exercise and occupy the art and faculty of playing comedies tragedies interludes stage plays and such other like as they have already used and studied or hereafter shall use and study as well for the recreation of our loving subjects as for our solace and pleasure."[3]

The establishment of the theatre in London as an institution protected by the law was the signal for a concerted attack by an alliance of burghers and clergy. The opening shot was fired by John Northbrooke, a Bristol clergyman. In a work entitled *Dicing, Dauncing, Vaine Playes, with other idle Pastimes, and commonly used on the Sabbath day, are reproved by the Authorities of the word of God and auntient writers,* Northbrooke revived the arguments used by the fathers of the church:

> If you will learne howe to bee false and deceyve your husbandes, or husbandes their wives, howe to playe the harlottes, to obtayne ones love, howe to ravishe, howe to beguyle, howe to betraye, to flatter, lye, sweare, forsweare, howe to allure to whoredome, howe to murther, howe to poyson, howe to disobey and rebell against princes, to consume treasures prodigally, to moove to lustes, to ransacke and spoyle cities and townes, to bee ydle, to blaspheme, to sing filthie songes of love, to speak filthily, to be prowde, howe to mocke, scoffe and deryde any nation . . . shall not you learne, then, at such enterludes howe to practice them?[4]

Theatres being such dens of iniquity, Northbrooke called upon the authorities to shut them down and to abolish the profession of actor. Like many churchmen before him, he openly admitted that the theatre competed with the church. Regular theatregoers would not deny, in his opinion, that they regard plays to be equal to sermons in the benefit they bestow, but much less taxing on the patience of listeners. Thus, the theatre had become unfair competition to church attendance.[5]

The Puritan literature attacking theatre and actors is voluminous and varied. The pamphleteers include such a character as Stephen Gossen, an Oxford scholar and playwright in his youth, who in his middle age saw the light, joined the church, and publicly repented his sins. In his *Schools of abuse, Containing a pleasant invective against Poets, Pipers, Plaiers, Jesters and such like Caterpillars of a Commonwealth*, he wrote with sorrow how his past sins continued to haunt him and how his infatuation with the theatre in the past misled his workers into almost daily visits to the theatre.[6] We know little about Gossen's plays, but they must have been written in a lively, witty style, judging by the flair he demonstrates for vivid writing:

> In our assemblies in playes in London, you shall see such heaving, and shooing, such ytching and shouldring, too sitte by the women; such care for their garments, that they bee not trode on; such eyes to their lappes, that no chippes light on them; such pillows to their backes, that they take no hurte; such masking in their eares, I knowe not what; such giving them pippens to passe the time; such playing at foote saunt without cardes; such ticking, such toying, such smiling, such winking, and such manning them home, when the sportes are ended.[7]

So much for women who frequented the theatre for professional purposes, a contention which was not too far from the truth, as witnessed by less prejudiced observers. But even decent women, suggested Gossen, are prone to seduction in the liberal atmosphere of the theatre and though he does not think all of them would be as weak as to succumb, none is immune to the influence.[8]

Gossen admitted that not all plays were sinful; some plays do not offend against decency and moral restraint. One of them was *The Jew*, showing the evils of usury. Another was *Catilins Conspiracies* which he elegantly called "a pig of my owne sow," meaning written by himself, which demonstrated how traitors met their punishment.[9]

Though he admitted that some players were honest and respectable citizens, Gossen saw the profession as a whole as consisting of beggars living on the generosity of hardworking men and sponging off society.[10]

When Gossen's book provoked a spate of angry replies, he countered with an apology meant to "whippe out those Doggs, which have barked at mee for writing the *Schools of Abuse*." His wrath by then knew no limits. Actors whom he had originally called beggars now became thieves; unlike common thieves who take money by force, actors do it by permission, that is, by means of court licenses. Going even beyond his earlier strictures on actors, he considered them to be the most dangerous persons alive.[11]

Another Puritan writer, Philip Stubbes, a layman known as the author of ballads and pamphlets, attacked apologists of the theatre who dared to suggest that they disseminate the eternal verities, just as the Church did. He claimed that this notion was little less than blasphemy since it compared the devil with the good Lord, and legitimized the transfer of people from the House of God to the halls of iniquity.[12]

Antony Mundy (or Munday), like Gossen a former playwright who saw the light, inveighed against the court and the nobility for giving their support and protection to players. To all previous arguments, he added an economic one: the nobility commit a kind of begging and thereby harm their credit by allowing their actors-retainers to move around the country and to be paid for performances by other gentlemen.[13]

The war against the theatre also played an important part in the famous Marprelate Controversy. This was a battle of pamphlets between an anonymous, and possibly composite, Puritan, written under the name Martin Marprelate, and the defenders of the established church. His violent, pungently witty attacks on the dignitaries of the establishment included abuse of the theatre, which prompted the establishment to engage literary men to write replies. Thus, while the authorities were vainly looking for the elusive Marprelate, three dramatists—John Lyly, Thomas Nashe, and Robert Greene—ground out pamphlet after pamphlet written in the same pungent style Marprelate employed. The affair came to a rather dramatic end when John Perry, a Welsh Puritan who financed the Marprelate pamphlets, was apprehended, tried for sedition, and duly hanged.

The first serious, massive reply to the vilifiers of the theatre appeared in 1612 with Thomas Heywood's *Apology for Actors*. Heywood was a well-known actor and a prolific playwright who, in his own words, had "an entire hand or at least a finger," in as many as two hundred and twenty plays, and had been called by Charles Lamb "sort of a prose Shakespeare." A Cambridge graduate, Heywood was fond of displaying his learning and, as a member of Queen Anne's Men, he also belonged to the elite of the acting profession. The book was beautifully printed and bound, introduced with verses in Greek and Latin, the "unworthy Worke" dedicated to the author's former master, the Earl of Worcester, as well as to his "good Friends and Fellowes the Citty Actors."

Heywood's chief purpose was to extoll the moral values of the theatre, in refutation of the Puritan's chief argument that the theatre teaches immorality. Going all the way back to the Greeks and the Romans, Heywood demonstrated how the theatre had always presented the great deeds of noble men, while upholding for scorn the misdeeds of knaves.

> What English blood, seeing the person of any bold Englishman presented, and doth huggs his fame, and hunnye at his valor, pursuing him in his enterprise with his best wishes, and as being wrapt in contemplation offers to him in his hart all prosperous performance, as if the personator was the man personated? . . . What coward, to see his countrymen valiant, would not be ashamed of his own cowardise? What English prince, should hee behold the true portraiture of that famous King Edward the Third, foraging France, taking so great a king captive in his owne country, quartering the English lyons with the French flower-delyce, and would not bee suddenly inflam'd with so royale a spectacle, being made apt and fit for the like achievement?[14]

Probably motivated by excessive zeal which made him overlook facts, Heywood argued that the disciples of Christ never had anything negative to say about actors and acting. For how could they have, the moral power of the theatre being so great that a woman in Amsterdam, who saw the English play *Four Sons of Aymon* in which a wife drives a nail into her husband's brain, was stricken with remorse and confessed that she had done the same years ago.

Heywood realized, of course, that some shows did not live up to such lofty standards, and that the theatre was even used for nefarious political purposes: "Now, to speake of some abuse lately crept into the quality, as an inveighing against the state, the court, the law, the citty, and their governments, with the particularizing of private men's humors (yet alive) noble-men, and others: I know it distastes many; neither do I any way approve it, not dare I by any means excuse it." In order to curb such abuses, Heywood proposed to institute "wise and juditiall censurers, before whom such complaints shall at any time hereafter come."[15]

Heywood's apology provoked a spate of counterattacks. One of them, entitled *A Refutation of the Apology of Actors*, by someone signing himself I. G., deplored the fact that by then (in 1615) acting was already a fairly well paying profession: "They find such sweet gains to maintain their idle life. . . . They give their whole industry. . . . Now at last, by giving two hours' vain babbling for as many hours' gathering of money, some of them become rich in the commonwealth."[16]

The actors' comparative affluence and their rising social status was an added source of irritation to the Puritans. A certain J. Cocke published an essay in which he mocked actors for putting on airs, pretending to be gentry: "His chiefe essence is a daily Counterfeit: He hath been familiar so long with outsides, that he professes himselfe (being unknowne) to be an apparent Gentleman. But his thinne Felt, and his silke Stockings, or his foule Linnen, and faire Doublet, doe (in him) bodily reveal the Broker: So beeing not suitable, hee proves a Motley.[17]

As the century and the reign of Queen Elizabeth were drawing to a close, the London theatres were well established and thus the actors were no longer satisfied with the academic rewrites of Latin dramatists or makeshift medleys. They commissioned, at handsome pay, plays from men of established reputation as poets. Thus the age witnessed the emergence of such dramatists of talent as Lodge, Lyly, Nashe, and Marlowe—the "university wits" as they were called. A minor member of that group was a bohemian character named Robert Greene, a graduate of both Oxford and Cambridge, which caused him to style himself "utriusque Academiae in Artibus Magister," a facile writer of poetry, plays, novels, and pamphlets. He also was a debauchee who died at the age of 34 in the house of a poor shoemaker to whom he owed money, following a banquet at which, according to a boon companion, he fell sick from overeating and overdrinking.

From his academic heights, Greene looked down at actors whom he favored by his plays, so much so that he thought nothing of selling the exclusive rights to a play to the Queen's Men, and when those went on tour, to the Admiral's Men. A true son of his period, which required each man to keep his place in the social structure, he saw playwriting as the sole province of people like him (university educated poets) and he resented actors trying their hands at writing plays.

In a pamphlet entitled *Greene's Groat's-worth of Wit bought with a Million of Repentance*, which came out soon after his untimely death, Greene attacked, without mentioning his object's name, one of those actors, calling him a bird beautified by foreign feathers, a tiger in sheepskin (player's hide), a self-styled versifier, and the like. And lest the "tyger's heart" taken from *Henry VI* not be sufficient to identify the upstart crow, Greene went on to describe him as "in his own conceyt the only shake-scene in a countrey."[18]

Thus the hack writer Robert Greene earned for himself a footnote in the history of British drama by his attack on Shakespeare. And the irony of it is that calling Shakespeare "a crow beautified with our feathers" turned out to be perfectly justifiable. About twenty years after Greene's death *The Winter's Tale* appeared, the comedy's plot taken almost in its entirety from a forgotten Greene play entitled *Pandasto, the Triumph of Time.*

The life of William Shakespeare, much as we know about it, is a fairly good indication of the relative respectability of the actor in the second half of the sixteenth century. He was born into a family of the middle class with distant connections to gentry, received a fairly sound education in the local grammar school, married at the age of eighteen a girl of similarly middle-class background, then dropped out of the sight of his future biographers for about a decade. In 1592 we find him in London, aged twenty-eight, working as an actor, playwright, poet, a member of the prestigious Chamberlain's Men company. We know little of his accomplishments as an actor, but we do know that he was by then already one of the company's chief suppliers of plays, delivering an average of two per year. His income from all his activities was quite substantial; estimates based on the records of the company range from a respectable £200 to a princely £600 per annum.

In the last years of his life Shakespeare seems to have been very busy fostering his social status. The house he built was the finest in town: he applied for and eventually was granted the right to display a coat of arms. He was buried in a manner becoming a distinguished citizen and churchgoer, in the chancel of the parish church. A bust showing him stiff, vacuous, and well barbered, watches over his grave in the Holy Trinity Church in Stratford.

Hostile sources spread exaggerated information on Shakespeare's affluence as well as of the affluence of other men of the theatre. *The*

Diary of John Ward, published after Shakespeare's death, alleges that in his later years, having gone back to Stratford, the playwright supplied the London stage with several plays and was paid about £1,000 a year for their performance.[19] And the renegade Gossen lamented the arrogance of actors who wore fine clothes and treated haughtily the very same men from whom they had taken "almes," being of course the price of the tickets.[20]

Robert Greene also resented the actors' prosperity; in the pamphlet in which he attacked Shakespeare he wrote resentfully of actors who only yesterday went from town to town carrying all their belongings on their backs, now being shareholders in companies where an actor's share in costumes alone was worth about £200. Some actors did indeed become very wealthy. Edward Alleyn, of whom Ben Jonson wrote that "as others speak, but only thou dost act," retired before he reached forty, bought himself a manor, and even established a college.

As for the majority of actors, it can be assumed that they earned a mere decent living, as the accounts of various companies would indicate. Permanent members of companies received their share of the profits, and when an actor retired he could sell his share and thus provide for his old age. Shareholding, however, by no means meant economic security; the company's income was subject to such catastrophies as plagues and riots which gave the municipalities the welcome opportunity to close the theatres temporarily. And during those periods the actors, in Ben Jonson's words, were "poorer, then so many starv'd snakes."

The moral and financial prosperity of actors in Elizabethan England was built on shifting sands. While the theatres enjoyed the protection of the Court and nobility, the Puritan forces persisted in their hostility, and in the 1620s those forces were becoming steadily more powerful. Municipalities used various pretexts to make it impossible or at least difficult for theatrical companies to perform within their jurisdiction. In 1623, the city of Norwich actually obtained from the Privy Council the right to ban shows altogether; the cities of Chester, Southhampton, and Worcester refused visiting companies the right to use public buildings; in other places actors were subject to the utter indignity of being paid a "gratuity" for leaving town without giving a performance.

In September 1642, the second month of the civil war, Parliament issued a decree banning all theatrical performances within the commonwealth because they were inconsistent with the grave state of the nation where "considerations of Repentance, Reconciliations and peace with God" were more in place than "Spectacles of pleasure, too commonly expressing lascivious Mirth and Levitie."

Six years later, the emergency decree was replaced by a decree proclaiming a permanent ban on spectacles of all sorts, regardless of licences issued by king or noble. The decree also called for the demolition of all theatre buildings, declared actors rogues and vagabonds, subject to public whipping should they attempt to practice their profession. Actors were reduced to dire poverty, and some previous members of theatre companies, including that of Shakespeare, lived to old age only to die destitute and in desolation.[21]

NOTES

1. Edmund K. Chambers, *The Elizabethan Stage*, vol. 4 (London: Oxford University Press, Clarendon Press, 1923), p. 324.
2. M. C. Bradbrook, *The Rise of the Common Player* (Cambridge: Harvard University Press, 1962), p. 53.
3. Ibid., p. 55.
4. Chambers, *Elizabethan Stage*, app. C, pp. 198-99.
5. Ibid., p. 198.
6. Ibid., p. 203.
7. Ibid.
8. Ibid., p. 205.
9. Ibid., p. 204.
10. Ibid., p. 205.
11. Ibid., p. 207.
12. Ibid., p. 222.
13. Ibid., p. 210.
14. Thomas Heywood, *An Apology for Actors* (1612) (New York: Garland, 1973), p. B4.
15. Ibid., p. G4.
16. Ibid., p. 4.
17. Chambers, *Elizabethan Stage*, pp. 255-56.
18. Ibid., pp. 241-42.
19. Ibid., p. 349.
20. Ibid., p. 204.
21. Ibid., p. 388.

5

The Bawdy
Restoration Theatre

If we go on in such Sins of Defyance,
may we not be afraid of the punishment
of Sodom, and that God should destroy
us with Fire and Brimstone.

Reverend Jeremy Collier,
*Short View of the Immorality and
Profaneness of the English Stage*

The Puritans had not succeeded in entirely extinguishing theatrical
life in England; under various guises, using all sort of means to
deceive the authorities, actors gave shows and people—the
common people and the nobility—went to see them. The shows
were, to be sure, mere shadows of the glories of the Elizabethan
theatre; many of the authors had been reduced to the state of vagabonds, and their performances reflected their lowly status. The
shows took place under the constant threat of police raids; an indignant chronicler described one such raid:

> The players at the Fortune in Golding Lane, who had oftentimes
> been complained of, and prohibited the acting of wanton and licen-
> tious Playes, yet persevering in their forbidden Art, this day there set
> a strong guard of Pikes and Muskets on both gates of the Play-
> house, and in the middle of their play they unexpectedly did press
> into the Stage upon them, who (amazed at these new Actors) it
> turned the Comedy into a Tragedy, and being plundered of all the
> richest of their clothes, they left nothing but their necessities now to
> act, and to learne a better life."[1]

Clandestine performances were given in private homes, at a tavern called the Red Hall, at a tennis court. Toward the end of the Commonwealth period shows were performed almost legally, thanks to a remarkable character who was destined to play the central role in England's theatrical life in the approaching Restoration period.

Sir William Davenant was a poet, courtier, adventurer, soldier, a ladies man with a knack for marrying wealthy widows, a wily unscrupulous operator who repeatedly found himself in trouble and always succeeded in extricating himself. His father was a prosperous Oxford vintner, his mother a beautiful woman; they frequently entertained distinguished visitors, one among them being William Shakespeare. The playwright's frequent visits to their home gave rise to the rumor that young William Davenant was his son. It is not known whether it was Davenant himself who started the rumor, but it is known that he cheerfully encouraged its currency.

Filial loyalty did not prevent Davenant from inflicting unspeakable indignities on Shakespeare's plays. John Downes in his *Roscius Anglicanus* describes a presentation of "the tragedy of Macbeth, alter'd by Sir William Davenant," in which the actors and stage were "drest in all it's Finery, as new cloath's, new Scenes, Machines, as flying for the Witches; with all the Singing and Dancing in it . . . it being all Excellently perform'd being in the nature of an Opera."[2]

A devoted royalist, Davenant somehow managed to maintain good relations with the Puritan regime, which allowed him to accomplish the almost incredible feat of maintaining what amounted to a string of theatres, in clear defiance of the law. He earned large sums of money from those enterprises, and even started to build a theatre, with the help of wealthy contributors, but the project was never completed.

In September 1656 Davenant presented *The Siege of Rhodes*, an "opera" he wrote. Skillfully driving a wedge into Puritan opposition, he gave the first performance as a semiprivate entertainment, careful to hire not actors but singers and musicians who did not legally come under the designation of rogues. Given a London population starved for entertainment, the show was a tremendous success. Thus encouraged, Davenant petitioned the authorities for permission to show "moral representations" which would help the government make their policies popular. Thus, when Cromwell was about to go to war with Spain, Davenant was allowed to present another opera, entitled *The Cruelty of Spaniards in Peru, Expressed by Instrumentall and Vocall Musick, and by Art of Perspective in Scenes, etc.* At the same time Davenant became involved in a royalist plot, was found out and put in jail but soon released. He was out just in time to welcome the returning Charles II who promptly commissioned him, along with Thomas Killigrew, to hire or build playhouses in London, and to start producing shows immediately.

Sir Thomas Killigrew was a minor dramatist, a wit, and a courtier of the exalted rank of Groom of the Bedchamber. The choice of courtiers to run the nation's theatres, Davenant at the Duke of York's House and Killigrew at the King's Servants, was characteristic of the nature of the Restoration theatre, as was the fact that the theatres were set up by royal fiat. Unlike the Elizabethan theatre, the Restoration theatre was meant for the upper classes rather than the common people. This, of course, determined the kind of plays performed, the staging, the acting, and the actors' social role.

The Restoration theatre was much more sophisticated and modern than its predecessor. The men responsible for the establishment and the tastemakers, the royal court and king, had spent a major part of their exile in the France of Louis XVI, had seen the Comédie Française with its elaborate scenery and costumes, its stage machinery and lighting. Back in England, they could no longer be satisfied with the comparative primitiveness of the Elizabethan stage. As a result, the theatre became more elaborate, the emphasis was on spectacle, the productions became costlier, and the entrance fee consequently higher.

One important feature of the Restoration theatre was the shift of emphasis from play to actor. The second part of the seventeenth century saw the beginning of the Age of Great Acting which came to its full flowering in the eighteenth century and continued through the nineteenth.

The audience went to the theatre to see the performance of a favorite actor rather than the play in which he performed; there were even connoisseurs who would see a show several times in order to distinguish the nuances, the subtle differences between one evening's performance and another.

One of those connoisseurs was Samuel Pepys to whom we owe a great deal of what is now known about the Restoration theatre, especially its social aspect. Though scholars harbor doubts about the accuracy of his information, and one cannot really rely on him for dates, names of persons, and of plays, his diaries are a cornucopia of information on the rich, brilliant, dissolute world of the theatre of his time.

Pepys was a man of humble origin; his father's family vaguely belonged to gentry, while his mother was a washerwoman. Intelligent and ambitious, Pepys managed to climb his way not only to the top of the civil service but also to high society, which made him a fearful snob; one can sense his delight in mentioning persons of title, the nobility and royalty he met, or only saw at a distance on his social rounds. By the same token the washerwoman's son frequently expressed his displeasure at seeing in the theatre common people marring the atmosphere with their appearance and behavior.

The theatre was a large part of the London social scene; one went there in the course of an evening's social rounds. A typical entry in Pepys's diary reads: ". . . the house being very full, and great company; among others Mrs. Steward, very fine, with her looks done up with puffs . . . and several other great ladies, and their hair so. . . . Here I saw my Lord Rochester and his lady, Mrs. Mallet, who hath after all this ado married him; and, as I hear some say in the pit, it is a great act of charity, for he hath no estate."[3] On another evening Pepys returned home from the theatre "not so well pleased with the company at the house to-day, which was full of citizens, there hardly being a gentleman or woman in the house."[4]

A major innovation of the Restoration theatre was the introduction of women to the stage, this too a lesson learned in France where women had been appearing for a long time. Also, practical considerations forced the theatres to employ women; the boys who had played women's parts before the axe fell were already grown men when the theatre was restored, and during the eighteen-year hiatus no new boys had received the necessary training.

With the Puritans looking over their shoulders, ready to pounce at what in their eyes was an infringement of morality, the Court saw fit to cloak the licensing of women performers in moral considerations. Thus the royal edict argued that,

> for as much as many plays formerly acted doe contain severall profane, obscene, and scurrillous passages, and the women's part therein have byn acted by men in the habit of women, at which some have taken offence, for the preventing of these abuses for the future . . . we doe likewise permit and give leave, that all the women's parts . . . may be performed by women soe long as their recreations, which by reason of the abuses aforesaid were scandalous and offensive, may by such reformation be esteemed not only harmless delight, but useful and instructive.[5]

The first actress to tread an English stage remains anonymous, but we know a good deal else about the history-making event. It took place on December 6, 1660, at the King's House; the play was *The Moor of Venice*. Aware of the importance of the event—Desdemona being played for the first time by a woman—the management had a piece of doggerel especially composed for the occasion. It was recited by an actor before the curtain rose and informed the audience that the part of the lady would in fact be performed by a woman and not by a man in female attire.[6]

There is no record of the public's reception of the lady, of the audience's reaction to the quality of her acting, or to the fact that a woman could do it at all. Unfortunately for posterity, Pepys was otherwise engaged that evening. We know this because about a month later he noted in his diary that he saw on that evening, for the first time in his life, a woman on the stage, in a play called *The Beggar's Bush*. The reason for his absence at the important event the month before might have been his low opinion of the play; elsewhere in his diary he unfavorably compares *The Moor of Venice* with *The Adventures of Five Hours* by Sir George Tuke.

(In order to remain safely on the side of historical accuracy, it must be noted here that a woman appeared on the English stage before Anonymous played Desdemona. She was a Mrs. Coleman who in 1656 appeared in Davenant's *Siege of Rhodes*. However, since she was an amateur who did not even memorize the few lines she had to say but read them from the script, and since she was never again seen on the stage, Mrs. Coleman is dismissed by theatre historians.)

Soon the English stage was swarming with women, much to the chagrin of the Puritans who saw here another reason for condemning the theatre as a nest of immorality. John Evelyn, another diarist and a man of sterner morals than Pepys, complained that "fowle and undecent women now (and never until now) are permitted to appeare & act, who inflaming severall young noblemen & gallants, became their misses, and to some of their wives," whereupon he listed a number of cases of noblemen marrying actresses.[7]

Indeed, the line separating actresses from "misses" was not quite clear; actresses, with few exceptions, came from the lowest strata of society, some of them directly from the brothels. They were a highly undisciplined lot, most with little talent and thus offering only their good looks and self confidence, and many made no pretense of separating their work on the stage from more lucrative pursuits in cavaliers' bedchambers.

One indication of the low esteem in which actresses were held was the free access to their dressing rooms—while they were in the act of dressing. Frequent incidents of swordplay between men vying for actresses' favors caused the king to issue a decree prohibiting gentlemen from visiting the "tiring rooms of the ladies of the King's theatre." The decree seems to have had little effect, as testified by Pepys who relates, in an entry dated six months after it was issued, how he spent a pleasant evening in the theatre where he met the actress Mrs. Knepp, "and she took us up into the tireing room: and to the women's shift, where Nell was dressing herself."[8]

Nell was, of course, Nell Gwynn, the most famous if not the most talented actress of the period. Brought up in a brothel, she moved a giant step up the social ladder when she was hired as an orange girl, a rather important position in the Restoration theatre. It meant not only selling oranges during the performance, but also acting as a go-between arranging liaisons of wealthy gentlemen with actresses. Nell's good looks and high spirits soon won her a small part in a play, from where she quickly moved ahead not only to reach stardom but, much more importantly, to become the king's mistress.

Nell never tried to hide her origin. On the contrary, she made a point of emphasizing it by the use of rough language no matter what the occasion, and she openly boasted about having come from the bottom of the social scale. We have it on Pepys's authority that when Beck Marshall, another actress, publicly called her Lord Buckhurst's whore, Nelly replied, "I was but one man's whore, though I was brought up in a bawdy house to fill strong waters to the guests; and you are a whore to three or four, though a Presbyter's praying daughter!"[9]

Her liaison with Lord Buckhurst, however, did not prevent pretty Nelly, as she was generally called, from giving birth, three years later, to a boy acknowledged by the king as his son and created Duke of Saint Albans; while Nell, who soon after retired from the stage, was rewarded for her services to the crown with the position of Lady of the Bedchamber to the ailing queen. Her ascent to such heights in the court hierarchy prompted Nell to compose her own epitaph:

> Here Nelly lies, who, though she lived a slattern
> Yet died a Princess acting in St. Cattrin.[10]

Nell Gwynn was the embodiment of the gay, bawdy Restoration comedy. To Dryden she was the ideal impersonator of his heroines; it was said that her personality greatly influenced their character. One of those was Florimell of *The Maiden Queene*; of Nell's acting in that part, Pepys wrote, "I never can hope ever to see the like done again, by man or woman."[11]

Another courtesan-actress was a lady with the unfortunate name of Bracegirdle. One of the ornaments of the Restoration stage, she was as beautiful as she was talented, and theatre managers knew well how to take the best advantage of her famous legs, making her appear in men's clothes, the legs encased in silk stockings. In the play *Marriage Hater Matched*, Anne Bracegirdle appeared on the stage expressing embarrassment at being so exposed, whereupon her partner assured her that her reputation was above reproach. "Oh, I am so ashamed," she would say blushing prettily, before launching into her opening speech.

Bracegirdle was not only the sex symbol of the Restoration stage but, according to the actor and diarist Colley Cibber, "she was not unguarded in her private life," never letting it be known which of the men who so enthusiastically applauded her was her current lover. "It was even a fashion among the Gay, the Young, to have a Taste or *Tendre* for Mrs. Bracegirdle," Cibber continues. "She inspired the best Authors to write for her, and two of them, when they gave her a Lover, in a Play, seem'd palpably to plead their own Passions, and make their private Court to her, in fictitious character."[12] One of her lovers, the handsome William Mountfort, an actor of whom Queen Mary is reputed to have said that he was so dangerous because he made vice look so alluring, paid with his life for the actress's favors. One night after the show, as he was about to enter her house, he was murdered by a rival who was the head of a gang of cutthroats. The murderer was arrested, but his name being Lord Mohun, and his victim a mere actor, he was given only a token sentence.

One eminent actress of the period was neither a sex symbol nor a courtesan. Mary Betterton started her career in a late version of Davenant's *Siege of Rhodes*, went on to play Ophelia opposite the celebrated Thomas Betterton who soon made her his wife, and became the greatest Shakespearean actress of the period, in a career that lasted a phenomenal thirty-five years.

In striking contrast to the lives of other actresses of her time, Mary Betterton lead the life of a respectable married woman, untouched by a breath of scandal. Even the gossip Pepys has nothing to say about her except to praise her acting. She retired at the age of fifty-four, and died at the age of seventy-one, two years after the death of her husband. Queen Anne, whom she had coached in elocution, granted her a pension—a gracious gesture but of symbolic value only because the pension was never paid. The actress must have been in financial straits shortly before her death; we have a record of a benefit performance given by the Drury Lane Theatre in 1711 for "the widow of the late Famous Tragedian, Mr. Betterton."

Mary Betterton was the last of the first generation of English actresses. When she died in 1712, the professional position of actresses was already firmly established. They had even become "sharers," that is, members of the companies who were entitled to their share of the evening's take, as testified by inestimable Pepys who once heard Nell Gwynn backstage swear like a trouper because the house was half empty that evening, and there was little to be expected at the "sharing table" after the show.

Mary Betterton could also be considered as belonging to the first generation of the Age of Great Actors, although she lived in the shadow of her actor husband Thomas, who dominated the English stage for almost half a century. The son of an undercook in the royal kitchen, Betterton had the luck to become apprenticed to a book seller who had been a wardrobe keeper at the Blackfriars, and retained his love for the theatre during the dark years. It was from him that Betterton learned the rudiments of acting, and his training was continued under Davenant. At the age of twenty-six he was given the star role in *The Siege of Rhodes*, which almost imme-diately established him as England's prime actor.

In October 1662, a little over a year after Betterton made his debut, Pepys noted in his diary that the actor was reputed to be a very sober, serious man, studious and humble, following his studies, and rich already with what he gets and saves.[13]

Betterton also had a high standing at court; Charles II, ever the Francophile, even sent him to France to study the theatre there so as to improve the theatre in England. The trip resulted in a number of innovations, the most important of which was the use of shifting scenery instead of the backdrops which had hitherto been used. In 1693 he was granted a royal license to set up a theatre of his own, a venture that failed after initial success.

Betterton was not a matinee idol. Anthony Aston, an otherwise admiring younger colleague described him as having "little eyes, and a broad face, a little pock-fretten, a corpulent body, and thick legs, with large feet." This did not prevent him from being the toast of London society where he stood out with his sobriety and high moral principles in the general debauchery that characterized the court circles.

Though he practiced a profession the Puritans considered inherently sinful, Betterton was a puritan at heart; he saw in the theatre primarily a means for disseminating moral teachings and fighting vice. Thus he expected actors in their private lives to live up to those lofty ideals. We hear him say in his biography that actors "who are vehicles, as I may call them, of these instructions, must contribute very much to the impression the fable and the moral will make. . . . For to hear virtue, religion, honor recommended by a prostitute, an atheist, or a rake, makes them a jest to many people, who would hear the same done with awe by persons of known reputation."[14]

The reputation and the behavior of his colleagues were quite distant from Betterton's ideal. The run-of-the-mill actors were a heavy drinking, fornicating, brawling lot. Rising in society, they adopted some of the worst habits of the gentry, including dueling. Swordplay among actors, between actors and spectators, and between actors and managers, backstage and in taverns, became such a problem that on May 5, 1698, the House of Lords took action in the matter, shocked by an incident in which a gentleman was wounded by an actor. The diarist Narcissus Luttrel reports that "the Lord Mounmouth moved the House against the impudence of the actors at the playhouses, upon Powell's wounding a gentleman; and the lords with their white staves are to desire his majestie that none of the players wear swords."[15]

The effect of the action taken by the House of Lords is recorded in the same diary, in an entry dated a year later. When bailiffs went to arrest an actor named Captain Hodgson for an unspecified offense, "the players comeing out in a body, beat and wounded them, and in the scuffle Captain Hodgson's man was cowardly run through the back by a bayliff, and immediately dyed, having nothing but a stick in his hand."[16]

Royal and noble patronage notwithstanding, the theatre was a place where the holder of a ticket in the pit was in danger of life and limb. While ladies of the nobility and their escorts in the boxes displayed courtly manners and court finery, young bloods and country gentlemen on a visit to the city were showing off their boorishness. In *The Country Gentlemen's Vade Mecum*, published in 1698, we find a vivid description of what the anonymous author considered a typical scene. When a group of country squires,

> to shew their Parts and their Courage, raise a Quarrel, and put the whole House into a Hurly-burly; then you'll see fine work, indeed; the Whores tumbling over the Seats, and the poor Squires and Beaus tumbling after 'em in a horrible fright, and disorder; the whole Pit's in Arms in a Minute, and every Man's Sword drawn, to defend himself; so that if the Uproar be not instantly supprest, 't is great odds but there's some body murder'd.[17]

The behavior of the public matched the behavior they saw on the stage. The diarist John Evelyn, who was not a member of the Puritan camp—and even wrote two plays which remained unproduced because he had no time "to write out faire and reforme" the scripts—wrote in 1663 that London had "more wretched & obscene playes permitted than in all the world besides," and he contended that "playes are now with us become a licentious excesse & a vice, & needs severe censors that should looke as well to their morality, as to their lines and numbers."[18] Five years later, having attended a performance of Dryden's *An Evening's Love, or the Mock Astrologer*, he confided to his diary that "it afflicted me to see how the stage was degenerated and polluted by ye licentious times."

Though Evelyn was one of the intellectual lights of his times, his opinions on the theatre had little impact, especially when compared with the formidable influence of a pamphlet by Reverend Jeremy Collier, a prominent divine. His *Short View of the Immorality and Profaneness of the English Stage*, published in 1697, started the so-called Collier Controversy and greatly contributed to a radical change in the theatre.

Unlike other ecclesiastical writers on the subject, Collier did not attack the theatre as such, only the theatre of his time; in the same vein as Betterton, he thought of the theatre as an instrument for the education of the people, which to him meant the propagation of the tenets of Christianity. What he saw instead in the contemporary English theatre was a cynical attitude toward morality, a great deal of obscenity, profanity, mockery of religion and of the clergy.

"The business of plays," Collier wrote, "is to recommend Vertue, and discountenance of Vice: to show the uncertainty of Human Greatness, and suddain Turns of Fate, and the Unhappy Conclusions of Violence and injustice; 'tis to expose the Singularities of Pride and Fancy, to make Folly and Falsehood contemptible, and to bring every Thing that is Ill under Infamy, and Neglect." Instead, he found and criticized actors for their "Smuttiness of Expression; their swearing, Profaneness, and Lewd Application of Scripture; Their Abuse of Clergy, Their making their top Characters Libertines, and giving them Success in their Debauchery."[19] With numerous examples and quotations from contemporary playwrights, he demonstrated that their plays delighted in debauchery and that they made women, even little girls, speak smut, for the greater delectation of their crude audiences.

In a play called *The Double Dealer*, "there are but four Ladies, and Three of the biggest of them are Whores. A great Compliment to Quality, to tell them there is not above a Quarter of the Honest!"[20] He found the prologues and epilogues even more offensive than the plays, because here "the Actors quit the Stage, and remove from Fiction into Life," that is, they freely mix with the audience, and the language used "would turn the Stomach of an ordinary Debauchee, and be almost nauseous in the Stews." As for moral lessons, the heroes of plays were contemptible characters, and were rewarded in the end for their misdeeds. In *Love for Love*, the leading character "is a Prodigal Debauchee, unnatural and profane, obscene, sawcy, and undutiful, and yet this Libertine is crown'd for the Man of Merit, has his Wishes thrown into his Lap, and makes the happy Exit."[21] His happy exit was with a girl who had an annual income of thirty thousand pounds.

Collier naturally objected to the invariably negative portrayals of clergymen on the stage. "To give some instances of their Civility: in the *Spanish Fryar*, Dominick is made a Pimp for Lorenzo; he is call'd a parcel of holy Guts and Garbage, and said to have Room in his Belly for the Church' steeple."[22] And in *The Provok'd Wife*, "Sir John Brute puts on the Habit of a Clergyman, counterfeits himself drunk, quarrels with the Constable, and is knock'd down and seiz'd. He rails, swears, curses, is lewd and profane to all Heights of Madness and Debauchery: the Officers and Justice break Jests upon him, and make him a sort of Representative of his Order."[23]

The attack was soon followed by another in Collier's *Dissuasive from the Play-House*. Dropping the fairly reasonable stance he had assumed in his first pamphlet, Collier here actually accused the theatre of being the cause of a violent storm, a disaster which wracked England in the days of September 26-27, 1703, inflicting many casualties and extensive damage to property. He concluded with a warning of worse to come: "If we go on in such Sins of Defyance, may we not be afraid of the punishment of Sodom, and that God should destroy us with Fire and Brimstone."[24]

Collier's attack on the theatre came at the waning of a period: the bourgeoisie with its puritan moral precepts was in the ascendance; the nobility with its lack of them was in retreat; and the theatre, ever sensitive to the spirit of the time, was changing. The witty, sophisticated, morally indifferent comedies of the early Restoration writers—plays like Wycherley's *The Country Wife* in which the hero circulated a story that he was impotent in order to find it easier to seduce women, or Congreve's *The Way of the World* which depicted a thoroughly corrupt, amoral society—were on their way out. They were being replaced by the sentimental, morally upright plays of Cibber and Farquhar, where profligates in the first act became repentants in the last one, having seen the errors of their ways and resolved to become upstanding, church-going family men.

Those plays catered to a new kind of audience, the common people who were filling the pits as they did in the days of Shakespeare. But the shopkeepers and the apprentices were of a different mentality than the commoners who went to the Globe. Years of puritan teaching had left their mark, and the ascending upright bourgeoisie expected their moral value to be reflected on the stage.

This audience was naturally much less sophisticated, and certainly less presentable-looking than the ladies and gentlemen of the court. Pepys was unhappy seeing ordinary apprentices and "mean people" being able to afford tickets at two shillings and sixpence apiece, and the playwright and critic John Dennis deplored the corruption of taste brought about by the influx of the nouveau riche.

"In the reign of Charles the Second," he recalled, "a considerable part of the Audience had such an Education as qualified them to judge of Comedy. That Reign of Pleasure, even the entertainments of their Closet were all delightful."[25] But now, he continued, the theatre has been invaded by "Several people who made their Fortunes in the late War, and who from a state of obscurity, and perhaps of misery, have risen to a condition of distinction and plenty. . . . In the present Reign, a great part of the Gentlemen have not leisure, because want throws them upon employment, and there are ten times more Gentlemen now in business, than there were in King Charles' Reign."[26]

One does not have to accept Dennis's aristocratic attitude in order to accept the fact that the rise of the middle class contributed to the deterioration of the English play. Except, perhaps, for the works of Sheridan and Goldsmith, English plays of the eighteenth century are of little distinction, and justly forgotten. Better remembered is the ephemeral art of the actor. Starting with the two Bettertons, England—and the West as well—had entered the Age of Great Acting.

NOTES

1. Leslie Hotson, *The Commonwealth and Restoration Stage* (Cambridge: Harvard University Press, 1928), p. 17.

2. John Downes, *Roscius Anglicanus* (1708), quoted in *The Restoration Stage*, ed. John I. McCollum (Westport, Conn.: Greenwood Press, 1973), p. 34.

3. Samuel Pepys quoted in McCollum, *Restoration Stage*, p. 151.

4. Helen McAfee, *Pepys on the Restoration Stage* (New York: Benjamin Bloom, 1916).

5. Rosamond Gilder, *Enter the Actress: The First Woman in the Theatre* (New York: Theatre Arts Books, 1960), p. 142.

6. Ibid., p. 141.

7. John Evelyn, *The Diary of John Evelyn*, vol. 3, ed. E. S. De Baer (London: Oxford University Press, Clarendon Press, 1955), p. 465.

8. McAfee, *Pepys on the Restoration Stage*, p. 251.

9. Ibid., p. 254.

10. Karl Mantzius, *A History of Theatrical Art in Ancient and Modern Times*, vol. 5, trans. Louise von Cossel (New York: Peter Smith, 1937).

11. McAfee, *Pepys on the Restoration Stage*, p. 244.

12. Colley Cibber, *An Apology for the Life of Colley Cibber* (London: J. M. Dent & Sons, 1914), p. 92.

13. McAfee, *Pepys on the Restoration Stage*, p. 240.

14. Charles Gildon, *The Life of Mr. Thomas Betterton the Late Eminent Tragedian, Wherein the Action and Utterance of the Stage, Bar and Pulpit are Distinctly Considered*, quoted in *Actors on Acting*, ed. Toby Cole and Helen Krich Chinoy (New York: Crown, 1970), p. 99.

15. Hotson, *Commonwealth and Restoration Stage*, p. 305.

16. Ibid.

17. Ibid., p. 304.

18. Evelyn, *Diary*, p. 510.

19. Jeremy Collier, *A Short View of the Immorality & Profaneness of the English Stage* (New York: Garland, 1972), p. 2.

20. Ibid., p. 12.

21. Ibid., p. 42.

22. Ibid., p. 98.

23. Ibid., p. 108.

24. Jeremy Collier, *Collier Tracts: 1703-1708* (New York: Garland, 1973), p. 15.

25. John Dennis, excerpted in A. M. Nagler, *A Source Book in Theatrical History* (New York: Dover, 1952), pp. 250-51.

26. Ibid., p. 252-53.

6

The Age of Great Actors

Take my advice; play drama for your own
pleasure, but never become a professional
actor. It is the finest, rarest, most
difficult of talents, but it is degraded
by barbarians and anathemized by hypocrites.

Voltaire to Lekain

It was the proudest century of Western civilization, the age of reason, the age of philosophers and of scientific discovery, of international trade on a scale hitherto unknown. It was the century of social foment culminating in the French Revolution.

It was also a great time for the theatre. As the eighteenth century dawned, theatre had been flourishing only in Italy, Spain, England, and France. While the rest of Europe from Germany eastward had only wandering troupes of the crudest kind entertaining the common people, the gentry had the benefit of French and Italian visiting companies. As the century came to a close, well-established, high-quality theatre was enjoyed by Germany, Poland, the Scandinavian countries, and even Russia which had been the slowest in assimilating the cultural progress of the West.

The eighteenth century was the century of the actor. No great playwright emerged, no new Shakespeares, Molières, Lope de Vegas, Racines, but we have the shining names of Adrienne Lecouvreur, Clairon, Lekain, Michel Baron, of David Garrick,

Sarah Siddons, Caroline Neuber, Friedrich Ludwig Schroeder, Konrad Ekhof—men and women of genius who revolutionized the art of acting and brought it to a height unheard of before.

It was also a century in which the acting profession assumed a new dignity. In the words of theatre historian Karl Mantzius: "Whereas in the first half of the 17th century the existence of such an art was not acknowledged at all, and in the latter part people began to realize that the representation of human character might be considered as an art in itself, in the 18th century this hitherto despised art was taken up as a subject for eager argument and philosophical discussion."[1]

The century produced voluminous literature on the art of acting, books written not only by the practitioners of the art but by philosophers, such as Pierre de Saint-Albine, and the protean Diderot. So highly was the art thought of, at least by its practitioners, that Michel Baron of the Comédie Française allowed himself to say: "In every century you may meet a Caesar, but it requires 2,000 years to produce a Baron."[2]

Actors also became acceptable in polite society; disregarding the still persisting official position of the church, the Abbé de Bellegarde wrote of actors as truly decent people, who are "frequented and respected by gentle folk in many quarters." Adrienne Lecouvreur kept a salon frequented by the cream of intellectuals and nobility; David Garrick rubbed shoulders with such intellectual and artistic lights as Samuel Johnson and Sir Joshua Reynolds.

Once they reached the upper stratum of their profession, actors were fairly well paid and enjoyed economic security. In France, one actress who had become a tenured member of the Comédie Française retired on a comfortable pension at an age that allowed her to enjoy it for twenty years.

Under the glamorous surface, however, the old prejudices persisted; society only exempted from opprobrium, partially, those whose names were dressed in fame. Colley Cibber, the British playwright, actor, manager, the author of the celebrated "Apology" for his life, deplored the fact that due to those prejudices the theatre was deprived of large sources of talent: "I am convinced, were it possible to take off the disgrace and prejudice, which custom has thrown upon the profession of an actor, many a well-known younger brother, and beauty of low fortune, would gladly have

adorn'd the theatre, who, by their not being able to brook such dishonour to their birth, have passed away their lives decently
unheeded and forgotten."[3]

To illustrate the point, Cibber told the story of a lady whose
titled family had abandoned her due to some "female indiscretion." Having found herself destitute, the lady intended to join a
theatre company, when an emissary of the family approached the
company manager with a warning not to accept her. "For here you
find her honest endeavour, to get bread from the stage, was looked
upon as an addition of new scandal to her former dishonour."[4]

In the eyes of the church actors remained beyond the pale,
regardless of their station in the profession; actors who had philosophers and princes sitting at their feet were still not allowed a
Christian burial. Adrienne Lecouvreur was buried in an unmarked
grave, as had been Molière fifty-seven years earlier. It took another
sixty years and a revolution to have those restrictions abolished.

Louis XIV took great interest in the Comédie, his own creation,
a bastion of French culture as he and his court saw it. The accent
was on elegance; the chief quality demanded of a performer was
perfect pronunciation. Also the actor's movements on the stage
reflected the elaborate elegance with which the nobility moved; his
costumes, with their profusion of lace and plumes, imposed on the
performer a highly artificial, balletlike mode of stage behavior.

It was a theatre cut to the measure of the world of fashion. The
common people did not attend the Comédie; for one thing, prices
were too high; for another, they would have found it boring. The
aristocracy went to the theatre to see and be seen, as well as to
enjoy the subtleties of the acting of their favorites. There were
those who attended night after night, if only to hear one mono-
logue, and to discuss the performer's inflections later in the evening
at a soirée. On any evening of the week one could find at the
Comédie the whole of the fashionable world, the ladies' attire
rivalling that of the actresses', dandified young aristocrats sitting
on the stage, close enough to touch the performers. It took the
determination and the formidable authority of Voltaire to free the
actors from the nuisance of stage audiences.

Being part of the world of fashion, actors became socially close
to that world; they were received by high society and entertained
high society in their own homes. Handsome and charming, the ex-

quisiteness of their manners and speech superior to that of their wellborn friends, actors were the darlings of society, supplying glamor to their gatherings. To quote Mantzius, "they no longer stood apart as a distant strange caste, who might indeed sometimes be allowed to appear among other people, but who could never count as anything but a sort of remarkable gipsy folk."[5]

Following the death of Louis XIV, a breath of fresh air was felt in France, and some social restrictions were relaxed. The Comédie Française, at that time the world's only known theatre with a permanent company, charged by law and custom with the task of perfecting the art of acting, was also allowed to introduce some changes. Acting had reached perfection of form, while becoming empty of contents. The more liberal regime of Louis XV who was, in addition, less concerned with the Comédie than his predecessor, offered the opportunity for reform.

One of those responsible for the change was Adrienne Lecouvreur who started her career shortly after the death of Louis XIV, in 1717. According to Voltaire, she "almost invented the art of speaking to the heart, and of showing feeling and truth where formerly had been shown little but artificiality and declamation."[6]

The life of Adrienne Lecouvreur is fraught with more drama than any of the plays in which she performed the tragic heroine. It offers an excellent illustration of the ambiguity of the actor's position after the profession had been granted some social acceptance.

Of distinctly humble origin—her father was a poor workingman —Adrienne Lecouvreur gained entry into the theatre thanks to the good offices of an aunt, a laundress who worked for M. Legrand, a *sociétaire* of the Comédie. A mediocre actor but a good teacher, Legrand was quick to realize that the girl was uncommonly talented, and took her under his wing. At the age of seventeen she made her debut in the Flemish town of Lille. It was during the War of the Spanish Succession. While the performance was in progress a shell fell close enough to the theatre to be heard clearly by the audience, but so entranced were the good people of Lille by the girl's acting that all remained in their seats!

Adrienne spent several years acting in various provincial theatres before she went to Paris for a debut at the Comédie, the event which marked a turning point in her life as well as in the history of

the Comédie and of French acting. It signalled the end of declamation, and the beginning of natural acting as the reigning style of the
Comédie.

Off stage, Adrienne Lecouvreur was a sparkling conversa-
tionalist who could hold her own with the most brilliant men of the
age, and whose company was sought by nobility. "It is the established fashion to have dinner or supper with me," she wrote in a
letter to a friend, "because some duchesses have shown me this
honor."[7]

In keeping with the customs of the day, the beautiful Adrienne
Lecouvreur was a courtesan. The luxurious "establishment" she
maintained, the large household with servants and carriages to rival
those of the duchesses who visited her, were not financed by her
earnings from the theatre, as they possibly could not, but by the
generosity of a succession of highborn, wealthy lovers. One of
them was simultaneously the lover of the Duchess of Boullion, who
tried to dispose of the actress by means of poison. The plot was discovered, however, the informer was thrown into jail, and all of
Paris was buzzing with the scandal. And since it would have been
impossible for a mere actress to take action against a Duchess,
Adrienne Lecouvreur chose her own way of revenge. During a performance of Racine's *Phèdre*, having discerned her rival in a box,
she stepped to the edge of the stage and looking directly at the
woman, recited the lines from the play:

> I know my baseness,
> Oenone, I'm not like those brazen women
> Who, tasting in their sins a peace serene,
> Dare flaunt a face where not a blush is seen.[8]

The audience at the Comédie understood perfectly well the
meaning of the scene, and there was thunderous applause. Several
months later the actress died after being stricken by a violent gastric
attack. There was no investigation of her death, and she was buried
at night in an unmarked grave. An indignant Voltaire called a meeting of the sociétaires to protest the shameful action, and a decision
was taken to go on strike. But the decision was never carried out.

Another bright star in the galaxy of French actresses produced during that remarkable period was Mlle Clairon. The illegitimate daughter of a seamstress and a passing soldier, she started out as a child actress in the provincial theatre, and arrived in Paris at the age of twenty, already well known, not so much for her acting as for the succession of fashionable lovers. She made her debut at the Comédie as Phèdre, and was instantly famous.

Claire Hippolyte de la Trude Clairon, a name she invented to match the dignity of a queen of tragedy, brought to her two professions a remarkable beauty which lasted well into her middle age. Oliver Goldsmith wrote that she had the most perfect figure of any woman he ever saw. A Parisian critic described her thus: "Her complexion is very fair, and her head is well poised on her neck. Her eyes are very large, full of fire and voluptuousness. Her mouth is adorned with beautiful teeth; her bust is well formed and heaves naturally. Her figure is lissome and easy in its movements, and her bearing very graceful."[9]

Having graduated from light operetta and comedy in provincial towns to the Comédie Française and grand tragedy, Mlle Clairon adopted a pompous manner which would have been ridiculous in a person of lesser self confidence. This did not prevent the people of Paris from discussing her amorous adventures in the wildest terms; an exceedingly coarse pamphlet by an anonymous author describing in detail her sordid love life before she reached her present heights was enjoying a lively sale. Her career lasted twenty-two years, following which she retired to lead a comfortable life among the riches she had accumulated, and keeping her connection with the theatre by training promising actors. She died at the age of eighty.

Of the male contingent, none shone brighter than Michel Baron who was literally born into the theatre, to actor parents. A pupil and protégé of Molière, he was the senior among the great contemporary actors, having debuted as a child long before Mme Lecouvreur and Mlle Clairon were born. At the age of thirty-eight, in the fullness of his talents, he retired, feeling that the exalted status he had achieved no longer permitted him to be merely an actor, and he devoted himself to writing plays, hoping that this would erase the stigma of the profession into which he was born. He wrote a number of frothy plays, one of which, *Le Rendezvous des Tuileries*, caused much amusement in Paris with its characters based on real-life actors and dandies. However, life away from the footlights proved to him unsatisfactory. He returned thirty years later, his voice slightly cracked but his physical appearance still impressive, to start at nearly seventy on a new acting career. Though Adrienne Lecouvreur is generally credited with the introduction of natural acting, it was in fact he who invented it, and Adrienne Lecouvreur was merely his most talented pupil.

The art of natural acting was still further advanced by Henri Louis Lekain, often called the last representative of the Age of Great Actors. In the elegant, effete world of the official French theatre he stands out like a barbarian, a natural force, a man who brought new life into the art he practised. It is no accident that the part for which he is most famous is that of Genghis Khan in a Voltaire play.

More than any other actor of the period, Lekain was a creation of Voltaire, discovered and trained by him to become the chief interpreter of Voltaire's characters.

Though his plays are now nearly forgotten, even in France, Voltaire was the most important playwright of the period, and was most often performed next to the hallowed trio of Corneille, Racine and Molière. Like the latter, he was also a director at a time when the profession hardly existed. In addition he was a fighter against the various discriminations suffered by actors; one of his accomplishments was doing away with spectators on the stage, a scourge against which Molière had vainly fought. The historic event took place on April 22, 1759. The playwright Charles Collé wrote on that occasion: "Theatrical illusion is now complete: we no longer behold Caesar about to knock the powder off a fop sitting in the front row."[10]

Lekain relates in his memoirs how he and the great man first met. The son of a fairly prosperous goldsmith, and expected to follow in the same trade, Lekain conceived at an early age a passion for the theatre, and joined an amateur troupe. Voltaire attended the troupe's performances and, impressed by the young man, asked him to visit him. When Lekain, full of trepidation, walked into Voltaire's house, the great man took him in his arms saying "thank God for creating a being who has touched me by reciting some tolerably bad verse.''[11] Though enthusiastic over the young man's talent, Voltaire warned him against abandoning the respectable trade of a goldsmith for that of an actor: "My dear friend, don't think of it! Take my advice; play drama for your own pleasure, but never become a professional actor. It is the finest, rarest, most difficult of talents, but it is degraded by barbarians and anathemized by hypocrites. The day will come when France will respect your art, but then there will no longer be a Baron, a Lecouvreur, a Dangeville.''[12]

Lekain had a difficult time establishing himself at the Comédie. Jealous of their hard-won social recognition, the sociétaires feared that the young man with his plebeian looks and uncouth manners would set them a century back. The struggle lasted fifteen months, Voltaire relentlessly championed Lekain, while Mlle Clairon, the Comédie's leading snob, headed the opposing faction. Another actor had applied for admission, and though he had a mediocre talent, his good looks and fine manners won him the admiration of Mme de Pompadour, the king's all-powerful mistress. Still, the king decided in Lekain's favor after he saw him perform. According to Lekain's memoirs, the king said to his Lord Chamberlain: "This man made me weep—I who never weep."

Lekain's homeliness—he was short, with bandy legs, and a flat, pimpled face—as well as lack of social graces made him an easy target for all the indignities suffered by his profession. A greatly sensitive man, he found consolation in frequent appearances abroad, especially in Germany where the court circles received him with the deference due a representative of French culture. It was those trips which, according to his friends, undermined his never robust health. He died in 1778, at the age of forty-nine, and with him the Age of Great Actors in France came to an end.

Across the channel, the Age of Great Actors began later and lasted much longer, spilling into the first third of the nineteenth century. It saw the emergence of a new kind of audience, the bourgeoisie with its newly acquired wealth and social status. Theophilus Cibber, son of the celebrated Colley, wrote in 1745 in a letter to Garrick on the audience in Covent Garden, one of London's two licensed playhouses: "Would you not acquaint such as may not have consider'd it, that the Metropolis is amazingly increas'd, that

Property is greatly diffus'd; that many Families are advanc'd; that all Degrees of People go to Plays, as the most rational Amusement; that there are near thirty times the Number of Spectators there were 30 years ago."[13]

Since London had only two licensed theatres, the Drury Lane and the Covent Garden, with a joint seating capacity of 3,500, tickets were at a premium. In his *Life of Johnson*, Boswell mentions that when he wanted to see Garrick as King Lear, he found the pit already full at 4:10 in the afternoon, about two and a half hours before the scheduled start of the show. For the opening of Sheridan's *The Discovery*, he and two friends arrived at four o'clock in the afternoon, placed their hats on three seats (there were no numbered, reserved seats in those days), and two went out to eat while he stayed on to watch and whiled away the time in conversation with Oliver Goldsmith.

The rise of a new wealthy class notwithstanding, England of the eighteenth century remained a rigidly stratified society, and this stratification was reflected in the order in which the audience was seated. Common people, apprentices, servants, sailors, soldiers, sat in the upper gallery; trades people sat in the "best" gallery, substantial burghers bought seats in the pit, while the gentry sat in boxes. The only ones who did not know their proper places were the pickpockets and the whores who could be found roaming the theatre.

As for actors, those who were not fortunate enough to be accepted in one of the two licensed London theatres had to struggle hard to survive. In London they were forced to use all manner of subterfuges so as to be able to perform, such as advertise a concert and throw in a theatrical performance. Some of those advertisements were quite transparent: "By the Wolverhampton Company of Comedians [at the theatre] this present Monday July 11 [1774] a Concert of Vocal and Instrumental music; between the Several Parts of the Concert will be played [gratis] the celebrated Comedy The West Indian."[14]

Outside London, actors had to lead their traditional wandering existence because no town could supply an audience large enough to support a company for a full season. Thus a company would stay in one place three months at the most, then move on, the actors walking behind the wagons which carried the scenery and costumes. They were a rather disreputable crowd; people locked their doors when they saw them arrive in town. There was the joke about an actor who was brought before a magistrate. When asked about his occupation, he answered that he played kings in tragedies, for which he got seven shillings a week and had to find his own jewels. A piece of doggerel in a periodical was more outspoken:

> A Pimping, Spunging, Idle Impious Race . . .
> A newst of Leachers worse than Sodom bore . . .
> Diseas'd, in Debt, and ev'ry Moment dun'd;
> By all Good Christians loath'd, and
> Their own Kindred shun'd.[15]

To counteract this public image of the profession, companies made efforts to recruit members whose background, appearance, and behavior were respectable. One advertisement called for "several actors and actresses, of character and address, who can make a genteel appearance in life." The candidates were assured that "the company's constant receipts admit of a livelihood superior to most that travel, and is conducted with as much regularity and decorum as a Theatre-Royal."[16]

There was certainly no lack of decorum in the licensed theatres in London where actors led fairly respectable lives, and the most famous among them was considered the peer of philosophers and statesmen. The man was, of course, David Garrick who revolutionized British acting as Michel Baron and Adrienne Lecouvreur had done in France, and who in the years 1741-1776 dominated the British stage like no one before him.

The son of an army officer, Garrick received a fairly good education, and started out in life as a businessman in partnership with a brother. Business failed because young David did not pay much attention to it, occupied as he was appearing in amateur theatricals and writing plays. He soon abandoned business altogether to devote himself to the stage. He made friends with the actor Charles Macklin and fell in love with the beautiful but irresponsible actress Peg Woffington, and the three set up a *ménage à trois*. This mode of life constituted a departure from prevalent social standards, but so was Garrick's choice of profession. He was well aware of this when he wrote to his brother and former business partner Peter: "Last night, I played Richard the Third to the surprise of every-body, and as I shall make very near £300 per annum by it, and as it is really what I dote upon, I am resolved to pursue it. . . . Though I know you will be much displeased at me, yet I hope when you find that I may have the genius of an actor without the vices, you will think less severe of me, and not be ashamed to own me for a brother."[17]

Garrick was an actor of extraordinary versatility; he could play tragedy and farce with the same vigor and the same astonishing identification with the character. He was of rather small stature but well built, and his movements were exceptionally beautiful—when he wanted them to be so. He was the first actor in England to give free rule to passion, which the public found so fascinating. As an actor, and in later years as the copatentee of the Drury Lane, he thoroughly revitalized English acting.

He was famous throughout the Western world. Even in France where anything not French was considered inferior, Garrick was feted by the intellectual elite, and Diderot's *Le Paradox de Comedien* is reputed to have been written as a result of having seen Garrick act and having heard him talk of his art.

As a theatre manager, Garrick was the personification of bour-geois virtues. His biographer Thomas Davies declared:

> Order, decency, and decorum were the first objects which our young manager kept constantly in his eye at the commencement of his administration. He was so accomplished himself in all the external behavior, as well as in the more valuable talents of his profession, that his example was greatly conducive to that regularity which he labored to establish. . . . Those players who had fallen into an unlucky habit of imperfection in their parts, and of being obliged to supply that defect by assuming a bold front, and forging matter of their own, Mr. Garrick steadily discouraged, till, by being laid aside for some time, they had learned to pay a proper respect to the audience and the author.[18]

It was also due to his immense prestige that he managed to accomplish what others before him tried and did not succeed at: banishing the fops and dandies from the stage where they occupied precious space and made a nuisance of themselves with their immoderate behavior. This happened in 1763, four years after Voltaire accomplished the same at the Comédie.

Garrick spent a great deal of time, effort, and money in cultivating his public image. The three volumes of his published correspondence as well as his unpublished, posthumously discovered letters reveal that he was involved in the editorial policy of some newspapers, that he owned stock in a number of them, and was not above bribing journalists to write well of him. He never let an attack in the press remain unanswered; he even wrote reviews of his own performances, as his widow confessed to Edmund Kean years after his death. He kept in his employ a certain Paul Hiffernan, nicknamed "Gallows Paul," a dubious character whose main job was to insert "puffs" in newspapers about Garrick. When Hiffernan published his five-volume collected writings on the theatre, most of which referred to Garrick, the latter rewarded him with a pension.

Garrick's vanity did not, however, prevent him from seeking out talent to match his. It was he who discovered Sarah Kemble, better known as Mrs. Siddons, who with her brother John Kemble represent the final flowering of the great age in England. Both Kembles were impeccably respectable persons. The daughter of a minor actress, Sarah married an actor, William Siddons, and for the rest of her life lived a quiet middle-class existence, with not a breath of scandal to mar it.

A great tragedienne, Sarah Siddons was known to be as dramatic offstage as she was when playing Lady Macbeth. It was said about her that she always spoke in blank verse. To an absent-minded waiter, she once said: "I asked for a porter, man, you bring me beer"; a saleswoman in a dress shop was asked: "This I like well, the cost, the cost?"

At the age of fifty-seven Sarah Siddons decided to retire in full glory. Her farewell performance, naturally as Lady Macbeth, was the greatest show she ever staged. In the packed Covent Garden, with tickets sold about six months ahead, the crowd rose to its feet and roared when she finished her sleepwalking scene, demanding that the show stop right there. The curtain descended, and the crowd roared for twenty more minutes, until it rose again to reveal the actress in a white dress, seated at a table. She stood up and recited an especially written farewell poem. After more applause, she was led off the stage by her brother John. And with her walked out of the British theatre the great tradition of eighteenth-century acting.

While the art of acting reached a peak and began to decline in England and France, the German theatre was still at the stage of folk primitivism. Unschooled, lowly vagabonds travelled from town to town, from village to village to display their bags of tricks, comic scenes combined with juggling and acrobatics. The companies were mainly extended families; it was the custom for actors to marry within the profession, because the travelling way of life demanded it; it would have been much too costly to pay the expenses of extra persons who did not contribute their labor.

The bands of actors were organized according to a rigid pattern, similar to that of the guilds in which crafts were organized, each member of the troupe having a set place in the hierarchy. The older actors treated the young ones as a master carpenter would treat an apprentice, using him as a personal servant, subjecting him to all sorts of indignities. The actors were badly paid, and worked very hard. An average company had to have as many as ninety plays in its repertoire.

Memorizing all those roles and playing night after night was only part of the actor's work; constant travelling called for a great amount of physical labor, and most of the burden fell on the young recruits to the profession. A book of German theatrical history contains a harrowing chronicle of a journey of a troupe to Denmark during an unusually severe winter, the sledges getting lost in the snowstorms, all the actors arriving at their destination suffering from frostbite.

We also find there descriptions of decor and costumes. The former consisted mainly of planks spread over barrels, a sheet of wallpaper used as a backdrop. As for costumes, we read of collars and cuffs cut out of paper.

The repertoire of those companies ranged from travesties of Shakespeare and Molière to pieces quickly stitched together by members of the troupe, this to avoid paying a playwright. As for the audiences, they were happy as long as they were given large portions of the perennial comic character Hanswurst, or of Pickleherring, a character who came to Germany from Holland.

Some of the plays' titles are fully revealing: *A schoolmaster murdered by Pickleherring or the Bacon Thieves taken in,* or *The World's great Monster or the Life and Death of the late Imperial General Wallenstein, Duke of Friedland, with Hanswurst.*

This native German theatre was for the common people only; the nobility had its own entertainment. Each of the little duchies and principalities into which Germany was divided maintained a court which strove to be another Versailles, and visiting provincial French companies frequently performed there.

The only native company known to rise above the Hanswurst-Pickleherring level was one organized by Johannes Velten. Unlike other company managers of the period, Velten did not come from the ranks of barbers or hernia surgeons; he was a well-educated man with diplomas from the universities of Wittenberg and Leipzig. We know little of the acting in Velten's company, which travelled all over Germany and Northern Europe, but the repertoire, with true translations from Molière, made by Velten himself, indicate that the company had higher aspirations.

It was not Velten, however, who started the German theatre on its road but a remarkable woman, Carolina Neuber, who almost single-handedly raised the theatre of her country from Hanswurst to a level equal to that of Western Europe. The daughter of a highly respected Saxon lawyer and civil servant who carried to extremes his German sense of discipline, the beautiful, spirited Carolina eloped at the age of fourteen with her father's law clerk. The two were caught and thrown into prison. After she was freed, Carolina spent another five years under her father's brutal care until she eloped again, this time more successfully, and together with her husband Johann Neuber joined a travelling theatre company.

The year was 1717, Carolina was nineteen years old and all she had to offer was her good looks, which seemed quite sufficient for the kind of theatre then prevailing in Germany. She was, however, of a far higher intelligence than the run-of-the-mill actresses and, of course, much better educated, having come from a higher stratum of society. During the ten years she and her husband spent travelling with various troupes, she developed a lifelong hatred for Hanswurst, the ubiquitous, vulgar, frequently obscene clown who popped up in every show to please the indiscriminating crowds; this hatred became the motivating force in her campaign for a good German theatre.

In 1724, Johann Christoph Gottsched, a scholar and translator of French drama into German, saw the company in which Carolina appeared, and wrote a pamphlet entitled *The Reasonable Censors*. The work is considered the first piece of theatre criticism ever written in German. Some of the ideas put forth in the pamphlet, aiming at a reform of the German theatre, were influenced by Carolina's acting. The actress and the critic eventually met, and after the company in which she appeared disbanded, Carolina formed a new one with Gottsched's aid and a new era in the German theatre began.

Gottsched was a pedant of the Prussian school who rigidly stuck to French pseudoclassicism and its strict rules. Goethe called him a fool, and Lessing said that Gottsched had less sense in his entire body than Hanswurst in his little finger. But he was a man of formidable influence, and he sincerely wanted to pull the German theatre out of the Hanswurst morass. Also, his translations of the French classical repertoire provided the material on which a new German theatre could be based.

Carolina Neuber's chief concern were the actors whom she knew as untutored and undisciplined, who never really bothered to learn their roles by heart, and thought nothing of improvising on the stage. She was the first director in the German theatre, the first to insist on careful pronunciation, to plan *mise en scènes* and choreographies of performances with large casts.

Out of her own sense of propriety and under the influence of the sternly moralistic Gottsched, Carolina Neuber also campaigned to make the actors' calling respectable, a pretty hard task at which she only partially succeeded. The unmarried actresses in her company were required to lead cloistered existences under her watchful eye, studying or sewing and embroidering in their leisure time, receiving their men friends only in the patroness's salon, under her chaperonage. Also, unmarried actors were constantly watched by the Neuber couple, and were ordered to stay away from taverns and gambling houses under pain of immediate dismissal. Marriages among members of the troupe were encouraged, and many couples lived happily under Carolina's maternal eye.

Carolina Neuber was a woman of protean talents. She was a versatile actress, the first in Germany to interpret the tragic heroines of Racine and Corneille, a highly effective comedienne in Molière's plays and in plays she had written herself. She was, above all, a great organizer with an extraordinary power of persuasion. In 1734, about ten years after she began to reform the German theatre, she fully dominated it. She accumulated titles, privileges, and patents, and had ducal courts competing for her services. She must have realized how unusual it was, in her era, for a woman to be in such a position of power, as this coy introduction she wrote for a programme brochure would indicate:

> Dear reader, here is something for you to read. To be sure, it is not written by a great, scholarly man. Oh, no! It is by a mere woman whose name you scarcely know and for whose station in life you have to look among the most humble of people, for she is nothing but an actress."[19]

Carolina Neuber was soon to find out that she was, indeed, nothing but an actress, all the honors notwithstanding. Having quarrelled with Gottsched, she had to disband her troupe. She formed a new one which did not last long, tried her luck as a hired actress in Vienna where her acting was found old-fashioned, wound up in Dresden living in a small room in someone's house where her husband of forty years fell ill and died. Soon after, old and destitute, she fell ill herself, on the road. A kindly peasant took care of her, after he overcame the revulsion of taking an actress into his decent home, and there she died. The good man buried her under the cover of night so that the local priest should not know an actress lay buried next to God-fearing folk. Sixteen years later, a monument to Carolina Neuber was erected on the highway near the hut where she found her last refuge.

Carolina Neuber's pupils went on to bigger and better things. The first generation of great German actors followed: Sophie Schroeder, Konrad Ackerman, Konrad Ekhoff. They all belonged to a company run by Johann Friedrich Schöenemann, a pupil of Carolina Neuber. True to her teachings, he too fought the Hanswurst comedy and strove for a better kind of repertoire. The company enjoyed the patronage of the Duke of Schwerin who bestowed on them the title of Court Comedians, but not much else for he could ill afford to subsidize them, and the company had to keep on struggling for existence. Ekhoff even set up a school for actors, the first one in Germany, but it soon closed. Dismayed by the sad state of the German theatre, the actor Friedrich Loewen, a son-in-law of Schöenemann, published a pamphlet in which he blamed everyone: the state, the company managers, the actors. Loewen's complaints found the sympathetic ear of a group of wealthy businessmen who established a new company with the best actors Germany then had, and the playwright Lessing was appointed resident literary adviser and editor of a theatrical journal, the first in Germany. The Hamburg National Theatre opened in 1767, and came to a sad end less than three years later. It was the first attempt in Germany to establish a theatre run on noncommercial lines and, though it failed, it had laid the foundation for others to follow.

It was in Hamburg where the art of natural acting was developed. The Hamburg theatre also offered the public a high-class repertoire based mainly on Shakespeare (eleven productions from 1776 to 1780). And Lessing, acting as the company's literary adviser and official critic, provided the theoretical foundations for the actor's art in his essays which became known as *The Hamburg Dramaturgy*. There he championed a fresh approach to acting in place of the French classicism that still held sway in the court theatres.

One of those court theatres occupies a very special place in the history of the German theatre, due to the man who headed it. Johann Wolfgang von Goethe, poet, dramatist, philosopher, scientist, the greatest figure of the century, was brought to Weimar by Duke Karl August, a man of intellectual aspirations that were not, however, matched by the size and the financial resources of his dukedom. It was the duke's ambition to transform the amateur theatre company of his court into a professional theatre, and it was for this purpose that he invited the great Goethe to Weimar. Goethe accepted because he saw there an opportunity to have his own plays performed under his own direction, and he also set about to turn the tiny court into a modern Athens, attracting some of the leading German poets and philosophers, among them Friedrich Schiller whose plays also received their first hearings there.

Aside from the repertoire, what with the dramas of Goethe and Schiller and Lessing, the Weimar company remained a small provincial theatre, run on a shoestring, the actors receiving parsimonious salaries. An official letter from the theatre's administrative director to Goethe states that "to buy a new dress [for the leading lady] would be too much. Perhaps she could make use of Mary Stuart's white satin dress; or the white satin dress in the wardrobe, the bodice of which Demoiselle Jagemann has recently been wearing, might be altered for the present purpose."[20] In another production, when the great Iffland gave a guest appearance in a role that called for him to swoon into a chair, there was no chair available, and the actor had to kneel instead.

The lack of proper scenery, costumes, and props meant little to Goethe who believed that all those things were of minor significance, the most important matter being acting. And he went about improving the acting with the zeal of a drill sergeant. He had every gesture of an actor thought out beforehand; he divided the stage into squares to which he related the performers' movements; and he sat at rehearsals with a baton, marking the rhythm of their speeches.

To Goethe the most important matter was pronunciation. One of his orders read: "His Serene Highness has been pleased to say that in future, whenever an actor fails to speak distinctly, His Highness himself will at once remind him of his duty." The soft wording carried a dire threat; an actress whose words did not reach the ducal box was placed under house arrest for a week and, to add injury to insult, had to pay the guard's fee. Severe punishment was also meted out to actors for other kinds of misbehavior. An actor was thrown into jail for beating his wife, for example. As Goethe explained it, the man was not punished for the act itself, wife beating being a private matter, but the lady was a member of the company, and as a result of her marital misunderstanding she showed up for a performance with two black eyes.

The director's dictatorial manner also extended to the audience. Strict regulations specified what was and what was not allowed; spectators were actually fined or even arrested for booing, for expressing their pleasure by other means than applause, or for laughing in the wrong places. At the premiere of Schlegel's *Alarcos*, thoroughly misunderstood by the audience who laughed during scenes intended to be serious, an enraged Goethe stood up in his box and thundered "Man lache nicht!"—no laughing allowed.

Goethe's reign over the Weimar theatre ended due to a dog. A play in which a dog played the leading role had been successfully touring Europe, and Frau Jaegermann, the duke's official mistress, wanted to engage him. Goethe strenuously objected, but the lady had her way, and he resigned.

Goethe had by then become an anachronism. As the century was drawing to a close, there were about seventy regularly functioning theatres throughout Germany, star performers were already the subject of mass adulation, many actors already led settled lives with a steady income and had achieved a degree of respectability and social acceptance. As for Hanswurst, he was relegated to the marketplaces, though here and there he reared his vulgar head in the respectable theatre. About half a century after Carolina Neuber's pathetic death, the seeds she had planted bore fruit.

Moving slowly eastward, the art of the stage reached Poland toward the end of the eighteenth century. However, another century had to pass before theatre became established there as an integral part of cultural life, and acting became a recognized profession.

The wealthy, cultured aristocracy of Poland spoke French, frequently visited France, and enjoyed the visits of French theatrical troupes along with those of Italian opera companies. It had also become fashionable among the wealthy landowners to maintain acting troupes on their estates made up of talented serfs, speaking of course the vernacular. Only in 1765 was the first public theatre in the Polish language established. This was due to the efforts of one dedicated man, Wojciech Boguslawski, who enjoyed the patronage of the puppet king Stanislaw August.

It was not a very auspicious beginning for a national theatre. The educated looked down upon it because it was not in French, while the uneducated had very little interest in the theatre altogether, and there was, of course, violent opposition on the part of the all-powerful Catholic clergy to the theatre and the actors. The king was powerful enough, however, to force the clergy to give a Christian burial to the beautiful young actress Anna Skurczynska who was taken ill during a performance and died soon after.

Of the beginnings of the theatre in Russia, we know that in 1672 Czar Aleksey Mikhailovich ordered a certain Colonel Nicholas von Staden to proceed to the Duke of Kurland and enlist there the services of, among others, musicians who were able to assist in staging comedies.[21]

Von Staden's attempt failed, since no experienced stage people were interested in going into the wilderness which was Russia, so the czar turned to one Johann Gottfried Grigori, a teacher in Moscow's German Village, a religious school. Having staged there shows with his pupils, Grigori was the only man in the capital with theatrical experience. And so, on October 6, 1673, a comedy based on the Book of Esther was performed in the czar's palace, and so pleased was the sovereign that he generously rewarded Master Gottfried, and ordered him to produce more plays. As for the actors, we learn that they were invited for an audience with the czar and allowed to kiss his hand. This distinction was granted to them in order to induce parents to allow their children to appear in plays. And indeed, a certain Kochetov who was about to disown his son for becoming a buffoon, on hearing of the honor bestowed on actors was reported to have taken the boy to Grigori, saying "let him be the Czar's comedian."[22]

While the honor was thus great, the material rewards were non-existent, as demonstrated in a heartbreaking petition submitted to the sovereign by "the humble subclerk Vaska Meshalkin and his colleagues." They had been sent to the German Village for training under Gottfried but received no salary or subsistence, wore out their clothes and boots, and were given nothing to eat and drink. The actors were humbly petitioning the czar that "a salary be granted for our daily food, so that, we thy slaves, serving in the profession of comedy, be not left to die of starvation."[23] The czar in his mercy granted them four halfpennies each day.

A quarter of a century later there was already a class of professional actors in Moscow, and their activities are well recorded, mainly in police and court books. An order issued by a magistrate states that "the comedian Shmaga, the drunkard who took by force some cloth from a merchant, shall be brought to the office and flogged with rods; henceforth he, as well as other actors, should they take part in any such trickery, shall be brought to the office and punished, each one according to his guilt, and the matter need not be reported to me."[24]

Shmaga, it seems, was no exception. Russian apprentice comedians carried swords illegally, some of them in their bare hands (without sword belts). They drank heavily, did not pay their debts to storekeepers, provoked noisy quarrels with others, and tried their hands at extortion. In the course of their attempts at extortion, they filed charges of slander against their victims, harassed them in court, but avoided places where they were known. The law suits were generally settled out of court, with considerable gain for the actors.[25]

The social position of actors and, one may assume, their public behavior improved after 1752 when the empress allowed performances to take place at the court in Petersburg, and even permitted several young, talented actors to enlist in the corps of cadets so as to improve their education. Four years later, an imperial theatre was inaugurated by order of the empress. Still, according to B. V. Varneke, the historian of the Russian theatre, even the court actors remained near the bottom of society. The upper classes treated them as lowly servants and the church persisted in its traditional condemnation of acting.[26]

The leading light of the period was Ivan Dmitrevsky whom the Russians compared to Lekain, Garrick, and Clairon. He was made Supervisor of Plays by the empress, which required him to teach aspiring actors, and he was handsomely paid for his efforts. However, according to Varneke, the general attitude toward the theatre remained nearly unchanged and contact with actors, even by famous and respected persons like Dmitrevsky, was considered an offense against etiquette.[27]

As a young man Dmitrevsky reluctantly played female roles because it was difficult to find women of talent ready to enter a profession that carried the stigma of disrepute. Theatre managers were also cautious in recruiting actresses, aware that every indiscretion of an actress would reflect on the profession as a whole. A certain Ivanova, a very popular actress, became the subject of a scandal due to her habitual drunkenness and promiscuity.

Fortunately for the theatre, there were the serfs, persons so low on the social scale that acting meant for them actual social advancement, in addition to freeing them from the drudgery to which they had been condemned by birth. Some of those serfs, male and female, started their careers by acting in their owner's private theatres, then made their way to the public theatres, and many a landowner discovered there a source of income. In 1793, the *Moscow News* carried the following advertisement:

> A girl of 16 for sale, a chambermaid possessing a good voice singing very skillfully, and therefore theatre lovers are hereby given

notice that the said girl can act cleverly in a theatrical part and also keep house and cook good meals.[28]

Whatever their image in the public eye, actors were already established professionals as the century was nearing its end. Those employed in state theatres were paid salaries according to a system of ranks, beginning with the leading tragic and comic lover, and ending with confidants. There were also pensions for retired actors and even for their orphaned children. However, it took another century for actors in Russia to gain a minimum of social acceptance.

NOTES

1. Karl Mantzius, *A History of Theatrical Art in Ancient and Modern Times*, vol. 4, trans. Louise von Cossel (New York: Peter Smith, 1937).

2. Ibid., p. 245.

3. Colley Cibber, *An Apology for the Life of Colley Cibber* (London: J. M. Dent & Sons, 1914), p. 44.

4. Ibid.

5. Mantzius, *History of Theatrical Art*, vol. 5, p. 230.

6. Quoted in *Actors on Acting*, ed. Toby Cole and Helen Krich Chinoy, (New York: Crown, 1970), p. 148.

7. Mantzius, *History of Theatrical Art*, vol. 5, p. 247.

8. Jean Racine, *Phèdre*, in *The Complete Plays of Jean Racine*, vol. 2, trans. Samuel Solomon (New York: Random House, 1967), p. 272.

9. Mantzius, *History of Theatrical Art*, vol. 5, p. 273.

10. Ibid.

11. Ibid., pp. 283-84.

12. Ibid., p. 284.

13. Cecil Price, *Theatre in the Age of Garrick* (Oxford: Basil Blackwell, 1973), p. 84.

14. Ibid., p. 176.

15. Ibid., p. 177.

16. Ibid.

17. Quoted in *Actors on Acting*, ed. Cole and Chinoy, p. 131.

18. John Foster, *Life of Oliver Goldsmith*, quoted in *Theatrical Criticism in London to 1795*, Charles Harold Gray (New York: Benjamin Bloom, 1964).

19. Rosamond Gilder, *Enter the Actress: The First Woman in the Theatre* (New York: Theatre Arts Books, 1960), p. 219.

20. Mantzius, *History of Theatrical Art*, vol. 6, p. 242.

21. B. V. Varneke, *A History of the Russian Theatre: Seventeenth through Nineteenth Centuries* (New York: Hafner Press, 1971), pp. 22-23.

22. Ibid., p. 27.

23. Ibid., p. 28.

24. Ibid., p. 39.

25. Ibid., p. 38.

26. Ibid., p. 72.

27. Ibid., p. 118.

28. Ibid., p. 106.

7

The Great Stage Controversy

Johnson:	True, Sir, Rousseau knows he is talking nonsense, and laughs at the world for staring at him.
Boswell:	How so, Sir?
Johnson:	Why, Sir, a man who talks nonsense so well, must know he is talking nonsense.

Boswell, *Life of Johnson*

In 1756, Geneva was a tranquil, prosperous city, an island of peace in the midst of war-torn Europe. The city was governed according to the rules laid down about two centuries earlier by Calvin, the great reformer; one of those rules was a ban on theatres.

The absence of theatres did not seem to bother the good citizens of Geneva, for we know of no clandestine performing groups there of the kind that functioned in other places where theatres were banned, such as in London of the Commonwealth. The one person known to have suffered from that lack was Voltaire. The philosopher and playwright who had dominated the French theatre before he earned the displeasure of Louis XV and, even worse, of Mme. Pompadour, was now living there.

Voltaire did not reside in Geneva proper, but on the outskirts of the city which were not within the jurisdiction of the republic of Geneva. His place of residence was Les Delices, a lavish estate he bought out of a fortune acquired in financial dealings which did not always meet the tests of legitimacy.

Living in the grand manner, holding court to Europe's greatest writers, intellectuals, and artists who went to Les Delices to pay him homage, carrying on a huge correspondence, Voltaire missed the living contact with the stage that had been so much a part of his life in his Paris days.

In a carefully planned but ultimately unsuccessful campaign, Voltaire began to stage theatricals on his estate, hoping thus to soften the hearts of the authorities and eventually bring about the abolition of the ban. He went as far as to invite Lekain, his former protégé and at the time the greatest French actor, to give a reading at Les Delices and, assisted by his niece-housekeeper, fed lines to the actor himself. Present at that event were all of the city's leading intellectuals and members of high society. "We made the whole State Council cry," he boasted in a letter to his friend d'Argental.¹ On another occasion Voltaire staged his own *Prodigal Child* with amateur actors drawn from local society. A number of clergymen attended, though they took the precaution of shedding their ecclesiastical garb for the occasion. However, when Voltaire staged another show, also a play of his own, *The Orphan of China*, the consistory got wise and forbade members of the clergy to attend.

It was at that juncture, in August 1756, that Jean Le Rond d'Alembert, the editor of the *Encyclopédie*, a formidable figure in the intellectual life of Europe who was a member of the French Academy as well as of learned societies in Prussia, Sweden, and Italy, arrived in Geneva to write an article on the city-republic for the *Encyclopédie*. This seemingly innocent assignment proved to have far-reaching consequences.

It remains unknown whether d'Alembert's visit was directly initiated by Voltaire, as it had been claimed by enemies of the two, but it seems reasonable to assume that the plea for the abolition of the ban on theatres which the article contained was inspired by the master of Les Delices even though, when the storm broke, Voltaire vehemently denied having any part in the matter. In a letter to a friend he wrote that should "any orthodox or heterodox person accuse me of having the slightest share in the article on Geneva, I urgently beg you to spread the truth. I have been the last to learn of the affair."² Veracity, however, never was the eminent philosopher's strong point. He once had his protector King Frederick of Prussia endorse an innocent pamphlet of his, then pasted the page with the endorsement on a pamphlet satirizing one of the king's ministers.

One of the persons who would not accept Voltaire's disclaimer was his one-time friend and protégé, Jean-Jacques Rousseau. A former member of that brilliant circle known as the *encyclopédists*, philosophers and scientists who had undertaken the formidable task of compiling the *Encyclopédie Française*, Rousseau had parted company with the *philosophes* for reasons not fully known but probably due to his unfortunate life-long tendency to alienate those who befriended him, and he missed no opportunity to attack them. In a letter to an associate Rousseau wrote: "I am not ignoring the fact that the article about Geneva belongs partly to M. Voltaire; I have been careful, however, not to say it. You will realize, after you read the article, that I know what I am talking about."[3]

A native of Geneva, though at the time living in France, Rousseau had every reason to be proud of the picture of his native city as painted by d'Alembert. The Frenchman found Geneva to be a model of good life and good government. The tiny republic was ruled by four syndics who were elected for one-year terms and could not be re-elected, and who strictly adhered to the stern but just laws set down by Calvin. The town was well lit at night, a rarity in Europe of the eighteenth century, and all citizens, rich and poor, had to walk on foot, vehicles being forbidden inside the city walls. Wearing jewellery and arranging ostentatious funerals also were forbidden. Peaceful among the constant wars ravaging Europe, Geneva was also, according to d'Alembert, a city of happy people. Nowhere else had he seen so many happy marriages with many children, the latter fact attributed by him to the ban on luxury which made child rearing easier. In addition to the city's prosperity, which was based chiefly on watchmaking, Geneva also claimed to be a centre of learning and the arts, attracting many distinguished foreigners. The only serious lack in the city's life, d'Alembert found, was the absence of a theatre which had been banned there chiefly because the authorities feared it would promote "the taste for adornment, dissipation, and libertinism which the actor troops disseminate among the youth." D'Alembert seemed to agree with those arguments, especially the one about the pernicious moral influence of actors, but he had a remedy to offer in the form of "laws that are severe and well administered concerning the conduct of the actors." Should Geneva adopt such laws, the city would have both a theatre and good morals. D'Alembert argued:

The barbarous prejudice against the actors' profession, the sort of abasement in which we have placed these men so necessary to the progress and support of the arts, is certainly one of the principal causes which contribute to the dissoluteness for which we reproach them. They seek to compensate themselves with pleasures for the esteem their estate cannot win them. Among us, an actor of morals is doubly to be respected, but we hardly take notice of him. . . . If the actors were not only tolerated in Geneva but were restrained by wise regulations, then protected and even respected when they had earned such respect, and, finally, placed absolutely on the same level as the other citizens, this city would soon have the advantage of possessing what is thought to be so rare and is only through our fault: a company of actors worthy of esteem.[4]

The ink was barely dry on the volume of the *Encyclopédie* with the article on Geneva when Jean-Jacques Rousseau published his open letter to d'Alembert, the most vicious attack on the theatre and actors of modern times, rivalling in its extremeness the invectives of the second-century fathers of the church.

Lettres sur les spectacles was violent, ill-tempered, in part brilliant and full of insight, in part illogical and self-contradictory, but a consistently eloquent piece of writing.

It came out in March 1758 in Amsterdam to cause a stormy Europewide debate which lasted about two years. The book was reprinted many times during Rousseau's lifetime and in the succeeding centuries, was translated into many languages and, incidentally, made more money for the author than any of his other, more substantial, works. A bibliography on the book lists more than four hundred items.

Part of the book's significance derives from the fact that, unlike other attacks of the kind, it came not from a clergyman but from a secular writer, and that it assaulted the theatre primarily on moral not religious grounds. There was also an element of piquancy in the fact that the author himself had written plays, and had been known, when he lived in Paris, to frequent the Comédie Française where he enjoyed the privilege of free admission, a valuable perquisite for a man permanently in financial straits.

The book was written at a time when Rousseau's fortunes were exceptionally low, which may partly account for its violent, hateful tone. He was living alone and in poverty at Montlouis, not far from the celebrated Hermitage of his former mistress, Mme d'Epinay, on the Montmorency estate, where he had spent happier days. That paradise was lost as a result of one of those tangled, eighteen-century love intrigues which involved his hostess, her sister-in-law Mme d'Houdedot for whom Rousseau conceived an unrequited passion, and a certain Baron Grimm, a German-born French writer.

In a footnote, Rousseau informs the reader that he wrote the book "without books, without memory, and without any materials other than a confused reminiscence of the observations that I have made in the theatre in the past."[5] It is difficult to take this claim seriously, considering the many lengthy quotations in Latin, and even more so seeing that Rousseau closely followed there some of the arguments advanced by Bossuet, the French prelate whose *Maxime sur la comédie* had been published sixty-four years earlier. The book was written in great haste, and immediately sent off to Rousseau's publisher in Amsterdam, with frequent letters following, badgering the publisher to hurry, another indication of the passion which made Rousseau write his attack on the theatre.

It is this passion which immediately strikes the reader, a passion extraordinary even for a man who charged all his writings with high emotion. Rousseau claimed to have composed the entire book in three weeks, which may very well be true. It reads as if written in one long, orgiastic session, the author pausing only to dip his quill in the inkstand.

There can be no doubt but the subject stirred up some powerful emotions in the author, which does not rule out, however, the theory held by some students of the subject that he wrote the book out of spite. Rousseau must have been well informed on Voltaire's campaign to re-establish theatre in Geneva, and it was probably no accident that the book appeared just when the squire of Les Delices was about to pull his biggest coup by sponsoring a company of actors in Carouge, in the territory of Savoy but on the very border of Geneva.

Rousseau's book was a boon to those who wanted to keep Geneva free of the scourge of the theatre. A prominent member of the local clergy, Pastor Moulton, wrote exultantly in a letter to his famous countryman: "Your book is the rallying cry of all good citizens here, the opprobrium and the terror of the wicked, and one may now judge of the greater or lesser love which each one bears toward his country by the degree of esteem that he gives to your work. In a word, if Geneva can preserve its former morals or recapture them, it is to you that she will owe it, and the palladium of this republic has issued from that article in the *Encyclopédie* which was to lead it to its ruin."[6]

Lettre sur les spectacles, or to give the book's full title, *J.-J. Rousseau, citoyen de Genève, a M. d'Alembert, de l'Académie française, sur son article Genève dans le septième volume de l'*Encyclopédie *et particulièrement sur le projet d'établir un théâtre de comédie en cette ville*, starts out with the full text of the part of d'Alembert's article dealing with the theatre. This is followed by the warning against the possible results of an article written by such a distinguished scholar and appearing in such a prestigious publication as the *Encyclopédie*.

"With what avidity will the young of Geneva, swept away by so weighty an authority, give themselves to ideas for which they already have only too great a penchant?" he asked in an all too clear reference to the campaign conducted by Voltaire. He continued:

> This is the subject of my alarm. This is the ill I would fend off. I do justice to the intention of M. d'Alembert; I hope he will do the same in regard to mine. I have no more desire to displease him than he to do us injury. But, finally, even if mistaken, must I not act and speak according to my conscience and my lights? Ought I have remained silent? Could I have, without betraying my duty and my country?"[7]

Evidently anticipating, and probably looking forward to the storm his book would stir up, Rousseau assumed the stance of a hero and a martyr for a cause. He told the reader how hard he found it to come out of "the sweet obscurity which was for thirty years my happiness," and how painful it was for him to part company with the *philosophes* in order to follow the dictates of his conscience.

D'Alembert, in Rousseau's opinion, avoided the basic issues. Questions which in d'Alembert's article seemed to have been answered were reopened. The value of the theatre itself, its morality, its suitability for a republic that abhorred luxury and, likewise, the moral standards of actresses and the effectiveness of laws in preventing the known abuses of theatre people—all of these were attacked by Rousseau.[8]

To answer those questions, Rousseau started out with the statement that the essence of the theatre being amusement, and amusement being necessary, one should seek it within one's family and community. "A father, a son, a husband, and a citizen have such cherished duties to fulfill that they are left nothing to give to boredom. . . . But it is discontent with one's self, the burden of idleness, the neglect of simple and natural tastes, that makes foreign amusement so necessary." Here Rousseau quoted the story related by Saint Chrysostom about the barbarian who was amazed to see Romans attending circuses and games. "Don't the Romans have wives and children?" he asked. The theatre is an escape, a means to evade one's duties. "It is there that they go to forget their friends, neighbors, and relations in order to concern themselves with fables, in order to cry for the misfortunes of the dead, or to laugh at the expense of the living."[9] Rather inconsistently, he suggested that the government of Geneva should provide such amusement as public festivals, sports contests, dances for the unmarried.

Admitting that tragedy may present positive moral values, he dismissed its moralizing effect on the grounds that the characters appearing there are so much larger than life, and their affairs so distant from our own experiences, that their example could not possibly instruct. And with characteristic lack of consistency he dismissed the Aristotelian theory about tragedy purging passions: "Tragedy purges passions one does not possess, while exciting those one does have."[10]

It is comedy, however, that he found dangerous, "the morals of which have an immediate relationship with ours, and whose characters resemble men more. It is all bad and pernicious; every aspect strikes home with the audience. And since the very pleasure of the comic is founded on a vice of the human heart, it is a consequence of this principle that the more the comedy is amusing and perfect, the more its effect is disastrous for morals."[11]

Giving Molière his due as "the most perfect comic actor whose works are known to us,"[12] Rousseau found his plays to be a school of vice, ridiculing goodness and simplicity while presenting treachery and falsehood in such a light as to arouse the audience's sympathy for the wrongdoers. Molière's evil characters are usually shown as clever and successful, while the good people appear to be fools, and consequently are victims. And while it is true in life that the good are the losers, should this be shown on the stage, with a tone of approval?

"See how this man Molière, for the sake of multiplying his jokes, shakes the whole order of society; how scandalously he overturns all the most sacred relations on which it is founded; how ridiculous he makes the respectable rights of fathers over their children, of husbands over their wives, of masters over their servants," comments Rousseau. Molière ridicules the miser, the snob, the jealous husband, but who does the public applaud if not the rascal who exploits their faults?[13]

True, miserliness and usury are great vices, but the conduct of the son toward his father is even more contemptible and vicious. An excellent joke may still be morally offensive.[14] Rousseau was shocked that at the time he was writing the authorities in Paris allowed the showing of a comedy that contained a scene in which a nephew, who had just witnessed his uncle's death, is busy pillaging the house instead of shedding bitter tears. All this is to the accompaniment of jokes exchanged by his unworthy companions. The most cherished duties and hallowed natural sentiments are trifled with and ridiculed, Rousseau declared.[15] He felt that in such scenes the audience identifies itself with the wrongdoers, "halfway taking part" in the action, and hopes that the mischief-maker—the thief— is not caught in the act.

He saw another detrimental aspect in the theatre's dealing so often with the subject of love. Love being largely the domain of women—since nature decreed that man is the aggressor and woman the resistor, and man can therefore achieve his aim at the expense of part of his liberty—such plays serve to make the position of women stronger, to influence the audience in the same manner the heroines exercise their charms over their stage lovers. "Do you think, Sir," he asked d'Alembert, "that this order is without difficulties; and that, in taking such effort to increase the ascendancy of women, men will be better governed for it?"[16]

The answer is, naturally, negative. Rousseau whose own love life had been both immensely complicated and largely unhappy, and who was at the time suffering from an unrequited passion, here took the opportunity to express his opinion on the fair sex: "Nature's most charming object, the one most able to touch a sensitive heart and to lead it to the good, is, I admit, an agreeable and virtuous woman. But where is this celestial object hiding itself? Is it not cruel to contemplate it with so much pleasure in the theatre, only to find such a different sort in society?''[17]

All this, however, was only preliminary. The book reached a climax with the discourse about the morals of actors. Dismissing out of hand d'Alembert's argument that especially enacted laws would improve actors' morals, he had some very strong opinions to express about those morals:

> To begin by observing the facts before reasoning about the cause, I see in general that the estate of the actor is one of license and bad morals; that the men are given to disorder; that the women lead a scandalous life; that both, avaricious and spendthrift at the same time, always overwhelmed by debts and always spending money in torrents, are as little controlled in their dissipation as they are scrupulous about the means to provide for them. I see, moreover, that in every country their profession is one that dishonors, that those who exercise it, excommunicated or not, are everywhere despised . . . this disdain is stronger everywhere the morals are purer, and there are innocent and simple countries where the actor's profession almost horrifies.[18]

To forestall the argument that the horror of actors was the product of the teachings of the church, Rousseau asserted that the opprobrium in which actors were held predated Christianity; it could be found in ancient Rome where actors were deprived of their citizens' rights, and actresses were classed as prostitutes. He admitted that actors were honored in Greece, and proposed a number of reasons for that, one of them being that since the Greeks invented both tragedy and comedy, they could not expose the persons of the actors to contempt, and when they came to understand the effects of this profession, the positive attitude had already become customary. And then, he casually remarked, Greece had never been an example of high morals.[19]

As for the cause of this prevalent disrespect in which actors were held, Rousseau saw it in the very nature of the profession:

> What is the art of the actor? It is the art of counterfeiting himself, of putting on another character than his own, of appearing different than he is, of becoming passionate in cold blood, of saying what he does not think as naturally as if he really did think it, and, finally, of

forgetting his own place by dint of taking another's. What is the profession of the actor? It is a trade in which he performs for money,
submits himself to the disgrace and the affronts that others buy the
right to give him, and puts his person publicly on sale. I beg every
sincere man to tell if he does not feel in the depths of his soul that
there is something servile and base in this traffic of oneself. You
philosophers, who have the pretention of being so far above prejudices, would you not all die of shame if, ignominiously gotten up as
kings, you had to take on in the eyes of the public a different role
than your own and expose your majesties to the jeers of the populace? What, then, is the spirit that the actor receives from his estate?
A mixture of abjectness, duplicity, ridiculous conceit, and disgraceful abasement which renders him fit for all sorts of roles except
for the most noble of all, that of man, which he abandons.[20]

And, he continued, wouldn't the skills he has learned in the profession carry over to the actor's private life?

Will these men, so well adorned, so well practiced in the tone of
gallantry and in the accents of passion, never abuse this art to seduce
young persons? Will these thieving valets, so subtle with tongue and
hand on the stage, never make a useful application of their art in the
interests of a profession more expensive than lucrative, will they
never have any useful distractions? Will they never take the purse of
a prodigal son or of an avaricious father for that of Leander or
Argan?"[21]

While actors' morals are low, the morals of actresses are even
lower. "But why is this dissoluteness of the actresses inevitable?
Oh, why! In any other time there would be no need to ask; but in
this age when prejudices reign so proudly and error gives itself the
name of philosophy, men besotted with their vain learning, have
closed their minds to the voice of reason and their hearts to that of
nature."[22]

After thus paying disrespect to his erstwhile associates, Rousseau
proceeded to explain what he saw as obvious:

There are no good morals for women outside of a withdrawn and
domestic life; if I say that the peaceful care of the family and the
home are their lot, that the dignity of their sex consists in modesty,
that shame and chasteness are inseparable from decency for them,
that when they seek for men's looks they are already letting them-

selves be corrupted by them, and that any woman who shows herself off disgraces herself; I will be immediately attacked by this philosophy of a day which is born and dies in the corner of a big city and wishes to smother the cry of nature and the unanimous voice of humankind.[23]

It took the *philosophes* much longer to reply to the attack than for Rousseau to have launched it. The task was assigned to Jean-François Marmontel, a member of the académie, an historian and author of minor tragedies. His reply came in the form of a series of articles in the prestigious *Mercure de France*, the first of which appeared in November 1758, eight months after Rousseau's book came off the press. The articles were later issued in book form under the title *Apologie du théâtre*.

It was a rather dry and flat book compared with the fiery eloquence of Rousseau's writing. It was also full of such sweeping and untrue statements as "the theatre condemns all pernicious inclinations," of "its aim is to unmask rascals and correct dupes."[24] Marmontel's chief argument was that, contrary to Rousseau's assertions, theatre fosters moral behavior by presenting evil actions in a light meant to warn the audiences against committing them, and that tragedy purges passions.

The same line of defense, though in a considerably more serious and better argued manner, was taken by d'Alembert himself when he decided to reply to the attack. "Tragedy," he wrote, "is morality in action, moral commands presented by examples."[25] As for comedy, here too morality is served by ridiculing evildoers. He agreed with Rousseau that actors, and even more so actresses, led immoral lives, but, reiterating what he had said in the original article, he laid the blame at the doors of society which forces them by its negative attitude and by unjust laws into a life of shame. And then, don't ladies of higher social position also commit immoral acts, this without the excuse of actresses who often have to do so in order to survive?

The debate lost some of its loftiness but gained in liveliness when a number of actors joined in. One of them, who signed himself P. A. Laval, Comédien, stated in the opening of his pamphlet that he wrote it in seventeen days (though it took much longer to have it published), and did so in order to counteract the poison (*une bile odieuse*) disseminated by Rousseau, especially the latter's portrayal of actors as "impudent, vicious rogues."[26] This, M. Laval asserted, sounds strange coming from a man known to have consigned his five children, born by a semiliterate peasant woman to whom he wasn't even legally married, to a house of foundlings.

Laval was followed by a certain Claude Villaret, a retired actor, who went to the extreme of maintaining that the theatre was indispensable to public morality, and if so, it follows that men and women engaged in the theatre ought to be highly moral persons. This he proved by pointing out that during the entire existence of theatre in France not one actor was executed for a crime. No other profession could make this claim, he stated.

Still another actor, a Prussian of French descent named L. H. Dancourt who established his respectability by dedicating the book to his sovereign, King Frederick, attacked Rousseau for making allegations without firsthand acquaintance with the subject, that is, the life of actors. And to prove how wrong Rousseau was, Dancourt gave a full account of his own impeccable life as a professional, family man, and citizen. He did admit that some actors were not above reproach but, like d'Alembert, he blamed bigoted society and unjust laws. As a professional, Dancourt was also able to inject a new argument into the debate: actors were often reduced to unethical and immoral acts because unscrupulous theatre managers made it impossible for them to earn a decent living.

The debate raged on. Another actor, a certain Jean-Jacques Le Boeuf argued in a pamphlet entitled *J. J. L. B. of Marseilles to his Friends, Concerning the Atrocities of the Paradoxes by the Contemptible J.-J. Rousseau*,[27] that actors were greater teachers of morals than clergymen, because the latter only preach morals while the former show them in action. And one Trebuchet maintained that the theatre was a "public school of atheism," and asked that it be exterminated as "the greatest enemy of the king and the entire human race."[28] Then there was the anonymous author of a book entitled *Tableau de Siecle* who advanced the theory that society's contemptuous attitude toward actors was merely a device meant to prevent members of nobility from marrying actresses who are more attractive than ladies of rank. This theory was taken up by the indefatigable L. H. Dancourt who published another pamphlet in which he suggested that actresses be recruited from nobility so that the social standing of the profession be raised.

It took about two years for the debate caused by the *Lettre sur les spectacles* to die down. Bibliographies of the subject list one final item, a brochure published by an anonymous priest in 1760, written in the form of a letter to Marmontel. The author asserted that the theatre is inherently immoral, which is proven by the fact that no moral play had yet been written. And it is this inherent immorality of the theatre which constitutes its chief attraction.

NOTES

1. Jean-Jacques Rousseau, *Lettre à M. D'Alembert sur les spectacles*, Editions Critique par M. Fuchs (Geneva, 1948), p. xvii.

2. Moses Barras, *The Stage Controversy in France from Corneille to Rousseau* (New York: Phaeton, 1933), pp. 257-58.

3. Jean-Jacques Rousseau, *Correspondance generale de J.-J. Rousseau,* vol. 4 (Paris: T. Dufour, 1925), p. 91.

4. Jean-Jacques Rousseau, *Politics and the Arts: Letter to M. D'Alembert on the Theatre*, trans. with notes and intro. by Allan Bloom (Glencoe, Ill.: Free Press, 1960), p. 4.

5. Ibid., p. 37n.

6. Barras, *Stage Controversy*, p. 258.

7. Rousseau, *Politics and the Arts*, p. 5.

8. Ibid., p. 15.

9. Ibid., p. 17.

10. Ibid., p. 22.

11. Ibid., p. 34.

12. Ibid.

13. Ibid., p. 35.

14. Ibid., pp. 35-36.

15. Ibid., p. 46.

16. Ibid., p. 47.

17. Ibid., pp. 47-48.

18. Ibid., pp. 75-76.

19. Ibid., p. 78.

20. Ibid., pp. 79-80.

21. Ibid., p. 80.

22. Ibid., p. 81.

23. Ibid., pp. 82-83.

24. Barras, *Stage Controversy*, p. 276.

25. Ibid., p. 279.

26. Ibid., p. 284.

27. Ibid., p. 297.

28. Ibid., p. 291n.

8

The Demoniac Actor

O! it offends me to the soul to hear a
robustius periwig-pated fellow tear a
passion to tatters, to very rags, to
split the ears of the groundlings.

Shakespeare, *Hamlet*

Goethe, the Romantic who saw himself as a Classicist, considered
Romanticism a disease; his contemporary Novalis, the quintessen-
tial Romantic poet, wrote of life as a disease of the soul. The good
citizens of London and Paris looked on with distaste at the young
men who paraded in the streets with hair flowing down to their
shoulders, their legs encased in velvet pantaloons. The première of
Victor Hugo's *Hernani*, the standard-bearing drama of Romanticism, was an occasion for riots.

One lasting achievement of the French Revolution was the break-
down of institutions and rules which had for centuries governed all
aspects of life, including the life of the arts. The individual asserted
himself, claiming the right to make his own rules, to govern himself
by his inner dictates. The Romantic poet no longer saw himself
bound to the sacred rules that came down from Aristoteles, the
dramatist disdained the sacred three unities, the clear demarcation
between lofty tragedy and earthbound comedy. Shakespeare with
his free mingling of high tragedy with low comedy, with his use of
the supernatural and irrational, was the model to be followed.

Art, to the Romantics, was the expression of the ultimate truth. As such it was superior to science and logic. The artist was not just an individual endowed with talent, but a creature apart, someone in league with supernatural powers, a medium through which those powers spoke to mortals.

The public expected of the artist, especially the performing artist, to live up to that image, and many an artist was cheerfully accommodating. Paganini took the best advantage of his naturally demoniac looks and of his extraordinarily long fingers which allowed him to perform feats on the violin no other virtuoso could attempt, and so enhanced the legend of being in league with Satan.

In Germany, the cradle of Romanticism, the actor became a mysterious, morbid creature from another world, a fright-inspiring figure on the stage where his performances often caused mass hysteria. Off stage, he was a dissolute, self-destructive individual, burning his candles at both ends, going down the path of madness and death, a slave of powers stronger than he.

While the actor of the eighteenth century arduously climbed the social ladder, striving to become a legitimate member of the middle class (with the upper crust of the profession actually achieving this goal), the actor of the early nineteenth century wrapped himself in a cloak of strangeness, disdained or appeared to disdain the advantages of the well-ordered life of a respectable burgher. August Wilhelm von Schlegel, the German theoretician of Romanticism, maintained that a settled life and financial security were incompatible with the actor's art. "The actor," he wrote, "with the equivocal way of life (which, in the very nature of things, it is impossible to alter) must be possessed by a certain reckless enthusiasm for his art, if he is to achieve the extraordinary."[1] Should the actor start worrying about such matters as salary and pension, his art will die. Wilhelm Tieck, another theoretician of German Romanticism, looked back with nostalgia to the days when all actors were gypsies travelling in wagons, independent of superintendents and other officials.

The paradigmatic Romantic actor in Germany was Ludwig Devrient. Possessed of a pale, intense face, burning eyes gazing from under a broad-brimmed hat, his gaunt body wrapped in a voluminous cloak, Devrient spent most of his free time in taverns where he ran up bills he was unable to pay, ruining his health and his talent, until he burnt himself out completely and died at the age of forty-eight.

Devrient entered the profession at the comparatively late age of twenty. After five years on the road, he appeared in his native city of Breslau as Franz Moor in Schiller's *The Robbers.* The performance became a sensation, Devrient won instant fame, and the role was associated with his name for many years to come.

The part of the evil Franz Moor seemed to be cut to Devrient's measure. Like Shakespeare's *Richard III,* Schiller's villain also had a repulsive malformed exterior which emphasized his satanic character. The role was customarily played by actors wearing wild wigs and an assortment of paddings in their costumes. Devrient discarded those devices; he could make himself satanically ugly without artificial aids.

According to a contemporary critic, in some of the dramatic scenes of the play the actor spoke "in accents not of this world." As for his facial expressions, there were "the eyes now flaming up in frenzy, now dying down into ashiness in the collapse of utter desperation—and the wild, Gorgon-like hair, with its loose locks twining about his forehead and neck like the snakes of the Furies—all this in terrifying combination formed a picture immeasurably far removed from what is ordinarily called acting."[2]

Devrient's closest friend and drinking companion for many years was E.T.A. Hoffman, the writer of gruesome, demonic tales. In his *Strange Sufferings of a Theatre Director* (in the course of his checkered career Hoffman was at one time a director of a theatre), he recounts his first meeting with Devrient, in a tavern of course. He saw the actor burst in, fling himself into a chair, order a bottle of champagne and a dozen oysters. He finished the champagne before the oysters arrived, all through the drinking talking to himself about his troubles, quickly emptying glass after glass as if trying to get drunk in the shortest time. Devrient was still a very young man, but his tangled locks were mottled with white, his face was pale and emaciated.

Given this appearance and character, it is no wonder that one of the achievements which won Devrient lasting fame was the mad scene in *King Lear*, a role at which he did not entirely succeed. He was only twenty-four when he undertook the task, and his small stature and unimpressive voice were considerable handicaps in portraying the giant among men.

But the final scenes seemed as if written for him. He threw himself into the part with a passion that taxed his physical powers, of which he had no abundance due to the manner of life he led. On one occasion he collapsed in an epilepsylike fit after the second act, so that the remainder of the performance had to be cancelled. An impressionable member of the audience thus described the episode in his memoirs: "The audience left quietly. I ran about in the street outside, driven by a deadly fear, keeping my eyes on the door by which the actors went out and in. . . . At last they brought him out, still dressed, in part, in the old king's costume. It was a strange scene. The disordered clothing, the pale face . . . it was as if they were carrying a dead man from the battle field.''[3]

In his mid-forties, Devrient was already a dying man, capable only of short-lived flashes. When he appeared in Vienna at the age of forty-four, an old admirer recorded his impressions in melancholy words:

> When I saw that rare being, with his head of genius and his eyes glowing with a feverish fire, sitting in his dressing room before the performance, languid and unstrung, his body shrunk together from nervous collapse and hardly under his own control; when we saw how mechanically he stretched out his arms and legs to his dresser to have the motley garments of his part put on him; it was hardly possible to conceive how this ruined frame could be capable of free artistic activity before the footlights.[4]

Devrient continued to perform intermittently, each appearance causing a sensation, people coming to see him out of morbid curiosity, expecting him to drop dead any moment. His death did come in the theatre, but backstage, after a performance.

In England, the Romantic actor was epitomized by Edmund Kean, an almost exact contemporary of Devrient. He was born in 1787, three years after the German, and died in 1833, one year after Devrient went to his untimely grave. Like the latter he led an offstage life that well matched his excesses on the stage, providing his public with all the vicarious thrills they were after.

Kean was the illegitimate son of a lunatic and a woman of loose morals. He grew up in the streets of London, received hardly any education or professional training, spent several years as a member of a company of strolling players or "commonwealth," as it was then called, and at the age of twenty-six astonished London with his portrayal of Shylock at the Drury Lane after only one rehearsal.

The nine years Kean had spent in the provinces were years of extreme hardship. In the commonwealths, the week's take was shared among the actors, but only after the manager deducted all the expenses, including his own salary. Quite frequently the share would amount to nothing, and the actors were reduced to starvation. The popular saying "take down the wash, the actors are coming" was based on some truth; one could expect anything from a band of starving people.

Almost every actor who appeared in one of London's three licensed theatres had his start in that cruel school, the only school where one could learn the rudiments of the craft. Only the chosen few made it to the London stages; the others remained in the provinces for the rest of their lives.

It was characteristic of Kean's attitude toward his profession that when he was already rich and famous he did not resent the suffering of the nine years on the road. At the height of fame, living in luxury, he was asked to testify before a Parliamentary committee set up to bring some order into the chaotic state of the English theatre, and he expressed there his opposition to the establishment of regular drama schools. He maintained that the only good schools were the strolling companies; they constituted a natural system of selection, so that only the best could reach London.

Hazlitt, who was then London's leading theatre critic and a great champion of the actor, described Kean as a little man with an inharmonious voice, with almost every physical disadvantage against him. As such, he was the exact opposite of John Philip Kemble, the outstanding personality of the English theatre until Kean's star rose.

Kemble was everything Kean was not. Handsome, with a dignified bearing, possessed of a melodious voice and beautiful pronunciation, he also led a highly respectable life and his social manners were impeccable. So were his stage manners; his sister, Mrs. Siddons, had said that in the most impetuous bursts he was always careful so as not to discompose his dress or his deportment.

Kemble was the embodiment of the respectability of the upper crust of the profession. But times had changed; the Romantic movement was in full flower, Byron and Shelley and Keats were the heroes in poetry, and the people looked for a similar hero on the stage. Edmund Kean who, in Hazlitt's famous phrase, played Shakespeare by flashes of lightning, had all the qualities of such an idol. Excessively emotional, eccentric, bent on self destruction, leading a life ridden with scandal, he played to the hilt the role assigned to him by society.

Not that he was not interested, as were those who preceded him, in rising in society; the bastard son of a strumpet and an itinerant alcoholic had his social ambitions. According to his biographers, when his appearance as Shylock brought the success it did, he ran home to his wife to tell her that soon she would be riding a carriage like all highborn ladies, and their son Charles would go to Eton.

At a time when the actor was all, one star performer could save a theatre from imminent collapse. When Kean was asked to join the Drury Lane, the company was on the verge of bankruptcy. In a dramatic reverse, the Drury Lane soon enjoyed unprecedented prosperity. Seats were sold out months ahead; all of London was anxious to see Edmund Kean as Shylock or as Richard III. For the second performance of the latter, after the enthusiastic reviews appeared, the public literally stormed the theatre.

Kean repaid the audience's enthusiasm not only with another great performance as the evil king but, in keeping with the image already established, fell ill the day after. Several days later, the following item appeared in the Morning Post:

> Mr. Kean has been extremely ill since last Saturday's performance. The great exertions requisite to sustain the part of Richard so much increased his disorder as to produce expectoration of blood. Dr. Pearson has in consequence been called in, and we are assured his report is favorable to a speedy recovery. It is even said he will be sufficiently well to appear again tomorrow in the arduous character of Richard. We trust he will not, unless he is fully recovered. The public are unusually interested in the success and recovery of this promising actor.[5]

The state of Kean's health became a frequent topic of conversation in London; the management of Drury Lane was accused of exploiting and physically ruining the actor. Things became so acute that Kean saw fit to publish in the press a letter to the manager of the theatre in which he denied those accusations, stating that he enjoyed perfect health, and was capable of appearing on the stage whenever and wherever needed.

Kean was the toast of London. Admirers sent him gifts of money and precious objects. The theatre management raised his salary to unprecedented heights, and this, together with the gifts and bonuses, soon made Kean a wealthy man.

When the first glorious season at the Drury Lane ended, Kean was besieged by offers from theatre managers throughout the country at fabulous fees. They wanted Shylock and Richard III, and Othello, but above all they wanted him to play Luke, the villian from a play entitled *Riches*, a shallow melodrama in which the hero commits all sorts of outrages before he meets his deserved end.

Public taste in London in the early nineteenth century was fairly low. The aristocracy was a selfish, reactionary, debauched lot, leading a life of ostentation, but still possessed of some taste. Socially, just below them was the up and coming bourgeoisie, their taste running to the sentimental and the moralistic. As for the masses, they were impoverished by the inflation and other economic ills brought on by the drawn-out war with Napoleon's France, and hardly counted as an audience. One must also remember that at the time more than two thirds of the English population was illiterate.

The behavior of the theatre public had improved since Restoration, but still when the German poet and critic Wilhelm Tieck visited a London theatre, he was shocked. We also have cartoons showing men fighting over seats in the gallery. And the situation was not much better in the boxes where the aristocracy sat. Byron habitually drank madeira and loudly cracked nuts during opening-night performances at the Drury Lane. And when Lord Cork, who had the reputation of a connoisseur of acting, honored Kean with a visit to see him play Othello, the actor noticed that all through the performance his lordship's children played hot cockles on the floor, much to their parents' amusement.

Byron and his circle of wellborn, fashionable friends took great interest in Edmund Kean, and the actor was frequently invited to their homes, though he was not much of a social asset. Morose and closed in, he spoke only when spoken to, and ostentatiously used the wrong forks.

Kean accepted those invitations mainly to placate his wife, a snob and social climber. He was well aware that he was invited only for the curiosity of it, and that he was expected to offer some entertainment in return. At small dinner parties he gave for his friends, Byron made him tell stories from his days as a strolling player, something Kean wanted to forget, or do imitations of Kemble and other famous actors of the day, which Kean did with the utmost reluctance.

Sensitive and egocentric as he was, Kean found another environment where he was sure to be the shining star. He spent much of his time in taverns, surrounded by sycophants and spongers. His drinking became a serious problem, often landing him in embarrassing situations. His highborn friends naturally knew of that other side of his social life, but this only stimulated their interest in him; it made him live up to the image of the eccentric, risen from the gutter to fame and riches but retaining his low tastes.

Kean's wife continued her social climbing. She even persuaded her husband to move from a prosperous middle-class neighborhood to Carges Street in the West End, an area inhabited by the most fashionable people, next door to a club so exclusive that the Duke of Wellington was once turned away from the door for wearing improper dress.

Kean's popularity reac..d a new high with his appearance in *A New Way to Pay Old Debts*, a melodrama by the Jacobean playwright Philip Massinger which featured what was probably the most villainous character ever conceived by a dramatist. It was the kind of part in which Kean particularly excelled. Critics wrote that what he did with the part went beyond mere acting; he had the audience speechless with terror. Ladies in the audience were fainting. Byron went into a fit.

Soon after, Kean received the first indication how fragile and fraught with peril was the position of an idol of the public. Having missed a performance in Brighton as a result of one of his customary debauches, he was replaced at the last moment by a young unknown named Junius Brutus Booth. The audience, which had started to boo hearing that Kean was not to appear, was soon so overwhelmed by the acting of the unknown player that the show ended with enthusiastic applause recalling Kean's first appearance as Shylock. News soon reached London that another Kean had risen and, striking while the iron was hot, Booth again invaded Kean's territory by playing Richard III at the rival Covent Garden, again with great success.

The rivalry between the two became a matter of keen interest to all of London, in fact, to all of England. The management of Drury Lane, ever on the lookout for increased profits, conceived the idea of stealing Booth away from the Covent Garden, and presenting the rivals on one bill in *Othello*, Kean playing the title role and Booth in the role of Iago. The performance took on the character of a boxing bout, bare-knuckled pugilism being a most popular spectator sport in England in those days. At the end of each scene the contenders shook hands like boxers after a round, and the audience cheered for one or the other. The *Morning Post* recorded the event in suitably sporting language:

> He [Booth] commenced his performance with great success. But as the play advanced he lost the high ground on which he had stood; and the comparison which the audience were increasingly called upon to make was not very favorable to him. . . . In some of the most interesting scenes his labours were witnessed with the most perfect serenity, and a most appalling calm prevailed where heretofore we have been accustomed to look for a storm of approbation. . . . With another actor in Othello, the Iago of the evening might have been thought great, but by the side of Kean we could discover in him nothing strikingly original in thought, vivid in conception or brilliant in execution.[6]

Tired of the constant struggle to maintain his position, Kean accepted an offer to tour the United States. He was received there with the respect due to England's most famous actor, but it took only one minor incident to bring into the open all the hatred puritanical America felt for actors. On his first visit to Boston Kean was very successful, but when the tour took him back there in the summer months, he found the audiences considerably smaller, and one night, when the curtain was about to go up on *Richard III*, he peeped through the hole to see only twenty people in the hall. He refused to play for such a small audience, and the hapless manager was forced to step out before the curtain and so inform the public.

The next morning the Boston newspapers exploded with anger. Kean was called an unprincipled vagabond who ought to be ridden out of town on a rail, or, as one newspaper suggested, to be taken by the nose and dragged out before the curtain to make his excuses to certain distinguished citizens who had honored with their presence the appearance of the little English actor. A Philadelphia newspaper demanded that Kean never again be permitted to appear in America.

The news spread throughout America, each newspaper trying to outdo the other in heaping abuse on the actor. He returned home and into the throes of another scandal, a much more serious one. Some time before his American tour he had established a liaison with a certain Charlotte Cox, the middle-aged wife of a socially prominent banker and, according to Kean's biographer, a thoroughly worthless woman. The romance was conducted almost in the open, under the very nose of her husband. The lovers frequently appeared in public together, and Charlotte even accompanied Kean on his out-of-town trips.

Ironically, the scandal erupted when the romance was already cooling off, to the point where the lady had taken another lover. Alderman Cox, who all during the romance had acted in a most complaisant manner, suddenly began to play the role of the injured husband by making a grotesque public scene. One evening, when Kean was presiding over a dinner in a fashionable hotel, Cox stationed himself outside and, brandishing a pistol, threatened to shoot the actor when he came out.

He did not kill the actor, but he did sue him for damages, and the trial understandably became the sensation of the day.

It was also one long protracted series of humiliations for Kean, especially when the counsel for the plaintiff read Kean's love letters in court to the titters of the audience. When the verdict was announced, awarding the cuckolded husband damages in the sum of £800, £1,200 less than he had sued for, the legitimate London press and the lower reaches of the publishing business exploded in an orgy of abuse. There were pornographic pamphlets with fabricated letters from Charlotte to Kean, replete with obscene details, and salacious cartoons showing the lovers in action. The August London *Times* had this to say: "It appears . . . that Kean . . . is advanced many steps in profligacy beyond the most profligate of his sisters and brethren on the stage. . . . It is of little consequence whether the character of King Richard or Othello be well or ill acted; but it is of importance that public feeling be not shocked, and public decency be not outraged."[7]

The "beyond the most profligate of his sisters and brethren of the stage" is characteristic. Kean was considered not only an immoral individual, but the most immoral one of an immoral lot. And an anonymous doggerel writer in the *Literary Gazette* gave vent to his outrage over a remark by Kean's lawyer made in court. Arguing that Kean's offense was a rather common one, the lawyer reminded the judge that the men at the royal court were also known for their loose morals. Those men, the doggerel writer spluttered, were gentlemen, unlike Kean, "Your client, bred to tumble for his meat / to act the monkey in plebeian street."[8]

All this was only the beginning. A week after the verdict, when Kean was scheduled to appear in *Richard III*, the manager of the Drury Lane discreetly suggested that the show be cancelled, lest there be disturbances in the theatre. Kean refused, and his act of courage was greeted by the *Times* with an article which claimed that the guilty man, "his offense aggravated by the most shocking circumstances of indecency, brutality, obscenity, perfidy and hypocrisy," was anxious to show himself to the public "because that very disgrace is calculated to excite the sympathies of the profligate and to fill the theatre with all that numerous class of morbidly curious idlers who flock to a play or an execution to see how a man looks when he is hanged, or deserves to be hanged."[9]

The newspaper's prediction was correct. Kean's performance did bring to the streets around the theatre a seething mass of the curious and of the violent who had to be kept in check by the police, while the hall was jammed an hour before the start of the performance. When Kean stepped on the stage, a mass shout went up to last all through the performance. They were screaming obscenities and throwing things on the stage while Kean and the other members of the cast went on playing. Not one word of what they said was heard.

Following the incident, the relentless *Times* published a still more brutal and revealing attack on the actor. It was the lead article. After an apology to the reader for dealing with so trivial a matter as theatre in so important a part of the newspaper, the editorial went on to suggest that since it was seemingly impossible to chase Edmund Kean off the stage, he should at least not be allowed to appear in love scenes; a woman unfortunate enough to have to earn her living on the stage should be protected from public contact with such a low creature.

There followed demonstrations in the streets when Kean appeared in the provinces, obscene attacks in the theatre halls. In Edinburgh, a group of respected citizens publicly stated that they would withdraw their patronage from the theatre should Kean be engaged.

Driven off the stage of the British Isles, Kean decided to try his luck in America again. It was a grievous mistake, for the American press had been faithfully reporting on the actor's trial, and his debut in New York was drowned in hisses and loud abuse. The next day, the newspapers came out with angry editorials against the appearance of that "lump of pollution" as one of the dailies called him, and asked of the American people to do their moral duty just as the people of London and Edinburgh had done it.

His spirits at their lowest, Kean appealed to the public for mercy. In an open letter he described himself as a broken man who came to the free land of America in order to seek shelter from his persecutors, and live out there the rest of his life in peace.

The letter had the desired effect. The sentimental side of the American character prevailed; he was allowed to perform in peace—in New York. But when he went to Boston, that citadel of puritanism, he met with the worst yet. As soon as his appearance was announced, rumors began circulating about impending riots. On the evening of the performance an ugly crowd milled around the theatre building, and when he appeared on the stage, he was pelted with eggs, nuts, and even heavy objects. In fear of his life, he had to get off the stage; he was smuggled out of the building past a bloodthirsty mob.

He returned to England in a poor state of health, facing an uncertain future. Fickle as ever, the public received his first appearance enthusiastically, but Kean was no longer the man he was.

Years of dissolute living and the recent troubles had taken their toll, affecting both his physical and mental health. No longer welcome in polite society, he again surrounded himself with sycophants and parasites, and acted foolishly in public.

It was already the beginning of the end. Kean was scheduled to appear in Thomas Colley Grattan's *Ben Nazir*, whose Saracen hero was the stuff of which great tragic roles are made. Rehearsals went on for a long time, everybody involved expected this to become the greatest role Kean ever played. Tickets were sold out weeks ahead and on opening night, when Kean, dressed in a magnificent Oriental costume, stepped on the stage, he was greeted with thunderous applause. But he did not remember a single line of his role. He muttered and stuttered, the curtain had to be brought down, and the performance cancelled. Kean was then thirty-nine.

He went on acting, with varying success, mainly in his old parts, Richard III, Othello, Sir Giles Overreach. Here and there the flashes of his genius were there to fascinate the public, but he was rapidly sinking into what one newspaper described as "premature debility of both body and mind." His behavior on and off stage became even more erratic, he took up with a woman of the worst reputation who fleeced him, and treated him with contempt in public.

On March 25, 1833, Kean performed in *Othello* at the Covent Garden. He delivered Othello's farewell speech with heartbreaking emotion and power which left the public stunned, whereupon he collapsed into the arms of his son Charles who played Iago, whispering "I am dying, speak to them for me," and was carried off the stage. He never regained consciousness in the forty days before he died. His estate amounted to £600 in debts.

The Romantic actor was late in arriving in France, as was Romanticism in the theatre. The revolution, which shattered existing institutions and broke venerable rules, somehow did not touch the theatre, perhaps because the French theatre had by then become so fossilized that no new life could be breathed into it. The establishment was headed by the Comédie Française; and the Comédie Française was run by the sociétaires, actors who had "arrived," and would do nothing to endanger their hard-won social respectability, their salaries and pensions. The revolution did touch on their lives in a most significant way; a 1791 decree ordered the church to abolish the ban on actors' eligibility for sacraments, so that from now on they could be married in church and buried in consecrated ground, that is, treated as human beings.

The younger actors of the Comédie, those who had not yet reached the exalted status of sociétaire, demanded that the theatre move with the times. The most important among them, both as an actor and as a forceful personality with definite political convictions, was Talma.

Talma first came to public attention in *Charles IX*, an indifferent play with political overtones dealing with the absolute monarch's massacre of the Huguenots. The sociétaires had only reluctantly agreed to the presentation of the play which, given the prevailing spirit of the time, became a great success with the public, as well as an occasion for demonstrations. When the sociétaires tried, under various pretexts, to take the play off the boards, riots broke out. Talma who fought the case of *Charles IX* became the hero of the day; the sociétaires expelled him, then were forced by public pressure to take him back; the theatre split and became paralyzed. The National Assembly passed a law cancelling the monopoly the Comédie Française had held until then, whereupon Talma and his followers left to form a new theatre.

The political disorder lasted for a number of years; some of the sociétaires who openly avowed their royalist sympathies were cast into jail and narrowly escaped the guillotine. Only in 1799 was order restored when Napoleon signed a decree under which the two rival companies were united. The Comédie regained its privileged position, complete with generous subsidies.

Talma was by then the undisputed king of the French stage, as well as a respected public figure, a personal friend of the emperor whom he reputedly tutored in regal behavior in public.

All this, however, did not win Talma a membership in the Légion d'Honneur, the common distinction awarded to men of achievement in all fields. With all his friendship and admiration for Talma, Napoleon could not bring himself to violate customs and so elevate an actor. In 1807, the playwright-actor Louis Picard had to give up acting in order to qualify for that distinction.

His failure to become a member of the Légion d'Honneur was not the only nor the worst insult Talma suffered. His two young sons, whom he enrolled in a fashionable school as befitting a man of his station and income, had won prizes. When it came to the award ceremony which was to be presided by the archbishop of Paris, the school authorities thought that the prelate would be reluctant to bestow the ceremonial kisses on the cheeks of sons of an actor, and the boys' prizes were reduced to honorable mentions.

Talma responded by removing the boys from the school. In a letter announcing this decision he wrote: "Until then I was unaware that the Catholic ban upon actors extended to their families." When the matter became public, and the royalist newspapers attacked the actor, he wrote in an open letter that "When the Lawgiver of the Christians called unto His little children for His blessings, He did not ask for their father's profession."[10]

Talma was born too early to become part of the Romantic age; his roots were in the classical French theatre, in the formal, elegant style of the Comédie Française. And though he introduced there a new, more natural form of acting, he was severely handicapped by the poor material in which he had to appear, the stilted tragedies of a bygone age, the shameful travesties of Shakespeare which ran rampant on the French stage in those days (a certain Ducis rewrote *Hamlet*—from a translation made by someone else, because, like all self-respecting Frenchmen, Ducis would not learn English—and decided to let the hero remain alive and marry Ophelia). Talma died a frustrated man. "I asked for Shakespeare," he complained in his old age, "and they gave me Ducis."

The French Romantic actor par excellence appeared at the time when Talma's career was about to end. He replaced Talma as the actor most admired by the public, but it was a different kind of admiration.

Frédérick Lemaître was the French counterpart of Devrient and Kean, an actor of genius who could amuse and frighten the public, a flamboyant character on and off stage, a man of a powerful though flawed talent, with the Romantic actor's bent for self-destruction. Though he lived to age seventy-six, his career was short; at a still young age he was a burnt out man, with no voice left.

Lemaître did not go through the customary routine of a French actor's schooling. He received his training as a circus performer, later appeared in pantomimes, and in the theatres of Paris's Boulevard du Crime, the street where every night innocent virgins met fates worse than death, hissing villains inflicted terrible punishment on their victims, fires and other disasters destroyed whole families. He became famous in something called *L'Auberge des Adrets* where he turned the character of the villain into a comedy part, making the people laugh instead of frightening them as it was intended by the author. Moreover, he changed the text at will every night, inventing new comedy lines and routines each time.

Like Kean in England and Devrient in Germany, Lemaître responded to the public's desire to see in the actor a demoniac character, a man inspired by supernatural powers, expressing passions of an intensity no ordinary man ever experienced. In one of his most famous roles he was a gambler in a melodrama entitled *Trente ans, ou la vie d'un joueur*, attracting Parisians over many months who went to the theatre to be frightened out of their minds.

Lemaître's female counterpart was Rachel who, in the words of the English critic George Henry Lewes, was a woman of "terrible beauty." The daughter of a Jewish peddler, she started out in life as a street singer. "There always seemed something not human about her," Lewes wrote. She stood and moved like a panther, a coiled spring always ready to leap.

Rachel was an actress of genius, but her range was narrow; she never even tried to tackle comedy and she was incapable of expressing feminine warmth. She was at her most powerful when portraying malignity, as in her most famous part of Phèdre in the Racine play. Women in the audience were fainting when they saw her possessed by the incestuous passion. To quote Lewes again, whoever saw Rachel play Phèdre would doubt whether he would ever see such acting again.

Off stage Rachel greatly resembled her heroines. She moved through life like a creature from another world, clad in her awe-inspiring beauty, consumed with a passion for money which she spent in a wildly extravagant way, exacting huge sums for her appearances, living at a fast pace of work and innumerable notorious amours, leaving ruined men in her wake.

One of Rachel's great successes was in the part of Adrienne Lecouvreur, in the play about the actress-courtesan where for many months she suffered and died every night of consumption. In a classic case of life imitating art, she contracted tuberculosis, and at the age of thirty-eight she died, in her own bed, as she had done innumerable times on the stage.

Across the continent, in Russia, actors were still treated as a better kind of servant, even though a number of them, like the great Mochalov who had been compared to Kean and Lemaître, were very popular. The majority of actors were recruited from the serf class, and they remained serfs even after they reached the heights of fame.

We have a vivid picture of the actors' status in Russian society early in the century in an essay by A. P. Karatygin, published as a preface to the diary of his father, the illustrious actor Wassily Andreyevich Karatygin. The nobility, we read there, treated all actors as buffoons, as a low breed of people whose job was to entertain them, while the female members of the profession were considered fair game for any nobleman. Liaisons between the latter and actresses were frequently arranged through the good offices of the theatre manager. Thus, an actress who enjoyed the favors of a powerful noble had a privileged position in the company, which meant primarily better parts, regardless of the woman's talent. Also, members of the company who would treat her with disrespect were likely to be severely punished. The company management had the right, at their own recognition, to punish an actor with fines, arrest, even public flogging.[11]

One way for an actor to eke out his miserly salary was a benefit, a greatly humiliating affair. The benefit would be announced several days in advance when, at the end of a performance, the company manager would present to the audience the beneficiary, and the latter would trot out his wife and children so that the good people would know how much he needed the money. On the day of the benefit, the actor, already dressed in his costume and accompanied by his family, would make the rounds of wealthy citizens and sell tickets.

What added to the low estate of actors was the snobbery of the upper classes who looked down on the Russian theatre, and patronized instead performances of visiting French troupes, whether they knew French or not. Russian actors complained that at a French performance there were long rows of six-horse teams in front of the theatres, while at a Russian show barely one could be seen.

The Moscow Company, an official theatre maintained by the crown and supervised by the governor general of the city, was composed mainly of serfs, most of whom the government purchased from nobles. The freedmen in the company were distinguished by the appellation "Mr." preceding their names in the programs.

There were not many freedmen in the company. No matter how low a person stood on the social scale, entering the acting profession meant stepping down a rung or two. According to a royal decree issued in 1827, government officials could become actors, subject to the permission of their superiors, but that deprived them of their rank, and their rank certificates were taken away from them.

In 1837 regulations were issued defining the duties of members of the imperial theatres, and the punishment for their violation. In addition to the already existing rights of the management to punish actors by fines, withholding of salaries, cancellation of contracts, and even arrests, the management was given the right to withhold the salaries of unmarried actresses who became pregnant, and of actors, male and female, who contracted venereal disease. On the brighter side, new regulations issued two years later specified that actors of the first category—there were three of them—were to acquire honorary personal citizenship after having served ten years, and hereditary citizenship after fifteen years of service.

It took many more years, the freeing of the slaves, and a revolution to make Russian actors full-fledged members of society.

NOTES

1. August Wilhelm von Schlegel, *Ueber Dramatische Kunst und Literatur*, quoted in Karl Mantzius, *A History of Theatrical Art in Ancient and Modern Times*, vol. 5, trans. Louise von Cossel (New York: Peter Smith, 1937), p. 287n.

2. August Klingemann, *Blumen und Ahrenlese,* quoted in Mantzius, *History of Theatrical Art*, pp. 319, 320.

3. Karl von Holtei, *Vierzig Jahre*, quoted in Mantzius, *History of Theatrical Art*, pp. 322-23.

4. Heinrich Eduard Anschuetz, quoted in Mantzius, *History of Theatrical Art*, p. 341.

5. Giles Playfair, *Kean: The Life and Paradox of the Great Actor* (London: Reinhardt & Evans, 1950), p. 104.

6. Ibid., p. 170.

7. Ibid., p. 239.

8. Ibid., p. 240.

9. Ibid., p. 241.

10. Herbert F. Collins, *Talma* (New York: Hill & Wang, 1964), pp. 315, 316.

11. B. V. Varneke, *A History of the Russian Theatre: Seventeenth through Nineteenth Centuries* (New York: Hafner Press, 1971), pp. 158-59.

9

Puritans and Hooligans in America

A nuisance in the earth, the very offal of society.

Dr. Timothy Dwight, President of Yale College

Nowhere in the Western world did the theatre find a reception more hostile than in the thirteen colonies which were to become the United States of America, a hostility which expressed itself in a variety of ways, and which has persisted, under a variety of guises, until this day. In the colonial times, and later in the first years of the republic, laws were enacted against the theatre, actors were declared outside the law and outside decent society. In later years, pastors and educators and statesmen spoke out against the theatre as a source of evil; in our times the theatre in America is the step-child of society as far as financial support is concerned, and the acting profession, the glamour and the riches of stars notwithstanding, is among the poorest paid, and leads all professions in unemployment rates.

Historians of the American theatre go back to the year 1665 when three men in Virginia had to face a judge for arranging an amateur theatrical performance of something called *Ye Bare and Ye Cubb* at Cowle's tavern near Punagoteague, Accomac County, Virginia. The judge found no law on the books under which he could convict the offenders, and so he only sent them on their way with an admonition.

We also know of plays performed at Harvard and other universities, but only as part of the curriculum, as an aid in preparing students for the ministry and public life. The same students, however, were punished for going to a theatrical performance outside the school.

In the early 1800s, the famous American educator Dr. Timothy Dwight, who as president of Yale proved himself a progressive with his encouragement of coeducation and the introduction of courses in the sciences, called actors "a nuisance in the earth, the very offal of society,"[1] and warned God-fearing people that by attending the theatre they would lose their immortal soul. And a generation later, when the theatre was already an established institution, the eminent Presbyterian pastor Dr. Theodore Cuyler of Brooklyn echoed those words in a language full of imagery when he described the theatre as a "chandeliered and ornamented hell—a yawning maelstrom of perdition—whose dark foundations rest on the murdered souls of hundreds."[2]

Those murdered souls belonged mainly to the lower strata of society; their social betters, especially the ladies among them, still shunned the theatre. "The most opulent and the most religious members of the community do not . . . approve of theatrical exhibitions," wrote an Englishman who visited New York in 1840. The theatres were crowded, but by "foreigners and persons who do not belong to either of the classes before enumerated."[3] And it took Harriet Beecher Stowe, a lady of impeccable social standing, several years to make up her mind to go to the theatre and see her *Uncle Tom's Cabin* performed.

The hostility toward the theatre, especially in New England, was to a large degree an imported attitude, an extension of English Puritanism, reinforced by the puritan attitudes of the early settlers whose raw life in a new and harsh country developed an enmity toward anything not connected with hard labor and the worship of God. Also, the Puritans who had migrated to America had done it at a time when the English theatre was licentious to the point of obscenity, so that theatre was in their minds an institution openly violating the principles of morality and godliness.

Not only the Puritans among the settlers opposed the theatre. The Dutch who had no such heritage, since theatre in Holland did not exist or hardly existed at the time they were leaving their mother country, were also hard-working people, and they demanded even harder work from their indentured servants; articles of indenture provided that an apprentice should not spend his time in alehouses and playhouses, lest this distract him from his duties, and make him spend foolishly the little money he earned.

The colonists' enmity toward theatre found an eloquent spokesman in the Quaker William Penn. In his *No Cross, No Crown*, Penn attacked the theatre as being opposed to the basic teachings of Christianity. "How many plays did Jesus Christ and his apostles recreate themselves at?" he asked. "What poets, romances, comedies, and the like did the apostles and the saints make or use to pass their time withal?" And when he founded Pennsylvania, which he envisioned as a "Holy Community" along the lines of the Quaker teachings, he incorporated in the law of the colony a provision prohibiting "prizes, stage plays, masques, revels, bull baitings, cockfighting."[4]

The first professional actor known to have breached the walls of the citadel of puritanism was one Anthony Aston. Appropriately enough, Aston was a vagabond, an adventurer, and generally a person of ill repute.

He was an Englishman, the son of a lawyer of whom it was said that "th' a lawyer, liv'd and dy'd an honest Man." The son received a fair education, and had originally intended to follow in his father's professional footsteps. He became instead a strolling player, and when he heard tales about the fabulous riches one could accumulate in Jamaica, he sailed for the New World. The Jamaica riches did not materialize, and so he proceeded to America, became a soldier, did poorly at that, and resumed his acting career. We have a record of that career, written by himself. "Well, we arriv'd in Charles Town," he wrote in his memoirs, "full of Lice, Shame, Poverty, Nakedness, and Hunger:—I turned Player and Poet, and wrote a Play on the subject of the Country." From there he went to New York, met there some old friends, and spent the winter "acting, writing, courting, fighting." Those occupations probably did not bring him the success he had wished for, and so he returned to Virginia, there scrounged up enough money for the passage back home. In England he again became a strolling player, travelling mostly alone, his cocky spirit never leaving him. In one newspaper notice he announced that "Disputation will be maintain'd against any or all, who are whimsical enough to oppose me on the premises."[5]

It seems that Aston's performances in New York found many emulators. Though no records have been preserved of their efforts, their existence is indicated by the fact that in 1709 the city council passed a law forbidding "play-acting and prize-fighting."

The reason why there are no records is that the newspapers and periodicals of those days shared the prevailing prejudices and ignored theatrical performances such as might have been taking place in New York. Having no access to newspapers, lacking the money for paid advertisements, the acting troupes or one-man performers advertised their shows by distributing handbills.

They had to battle constant official and popular opposition. Official America, the South to some degree excluded, was dead set against allowing the theatre to invade their God-fearing land. In 1750 the General Court of Massachusetts passed an act banning the theatre and all other kinds of public entertainment; in 1759 the House of Representatives of the colony of Pennsylvania passed a similar law, with the penalty for breaking it an astronomic £500; in 1761, Rhode Island followed suit; in 1762, the House of Representatives of New Hampshire banned an acting company on the ground that the theatre had a "peculiar influence on the minds of young people, and greatly endanger their morals by giving them a taste for intriguing, amusement and pleasure."[6]

Undeterred, actors applied various devices to make the theatre look respectable, and to circumvent the law. Typically, a performance would be introduced by an actor reciting a poem that justified the play as being moral and humane, and disputed the contemptuous attitude toward the theatre.[7]

A play called *The Gambler* was billed as a "Lecture on the Vice of Gambling"; *She Stoops to Conquer* was a "Lecture on the Disadvantages of Improper Education, Exemplified in the History of Tony Lumpkin"; a performance of *Othello* became a "moral drama," in which "Mrs. Morris will represent a young and virtuous wife, who being wrongfully suspected, gets smothered [in an adjoining room] by her husband." With an appeal added: "Reader attend: and ere thou goest hence, let fall a tear to hapless innocence."[8]

The first company of actors in America of which some records, although scant ones, have been preserved was the Walter Murray-Thomas Kean troupe, English actors who in 1749 made their first appearance in William Plumstead's warehouse in Philadelphia, from there moved to New York where they performed in another warehouse for over a year, later performed with little success in Williamsburg, gave one-nights stands all over the South, and, tired of starving, disbanded in 1752. When they gave a show in Fredericksburg, their audience included a twenty-year-old plantation owner named George Washington.

The Murray-Kean company's debut in Philadelphia is mentioned in the diary of the Quaker leader John Smith. He had dropped in for a cup of tea with a friend, and was shocked to hear that the man's daughter was planning to attend a theatrical performance that evening. He recorded in his diary that on that occasion he "expressed my sorrow that any thing of the kind was Encouraged."[9] Another local girl became so enamored with the theatre that she actually joined the company, much to the distress of her parents and the shock of their neighbors. It must have been this unfortunate incident which prompted the common council of the city to take action. The council had no authority to ban performances; all they could do was pass a resolution condemning theatre which "would be attended with very Mischievous Effects," the actors soliciting money "from weak and inconsiderate People" who would be taking bread out of the mouths of their children.[10] The city magistrates also warned the actors to behave properly while in town.

The Murray-Kean company was better received in New York; the press paid them some attention, so we know more about their sojourn there. To placate the moralists, the company gave a benefit for a local charity school. They performed *Richard III*, a play "wrote originally by Shakespeare," adapted by Colley Cibber. It being winter, they asked the audience to bring along little stoves. Benefits, they discovered, were attracting large audiences, so benefit followed benefit, one of them for a member of the company, a widow "having met divers late hardship and misfortunes."

As the company's receipts declined with the advent of hot weather, a number of the actors left to follow more profitable pursuits. A certain John Tremain advertised in the *Weekly Postboy* that he was giving up the stage in favor of cabinet making, and would sell his products very cheaply.

Little as we know of the professionalism of the Murray-Kean company—the scant notices in the press are unreliable, written as they were by journalists whose understanding of the theatre was for obvious reasons meagre—we can easily assume that it was not high, that the actors had had no proper schooling and no experience in real professional theatre.

The first theatre company in America that could be considered professional, not only in the sense that the actors made a living, such as it was, out of acting, was the Hallam company. It is their first American appearance that many historians of the American theatre consider the beginning of the theatre in the New World.

The Hallams, Adam and his four sons, had been minor actors in England, barely eking out a living there, when they heard that the streets in the New World were paved with gold. The company was organized under the management of brother Lewis, and in the spring of 1752, a boat appropriately named *Charming Sally* landed in Virginia carrying the entire Hallam family plus seven other actors and two actress wives, as well as a repertory of no less than twenty-four plays. They opened in Williamsburg with *The Merchant of Venice*.

The people of Virginia did not share the prejudices of their northern compatriots. They were also better cultivated than the Yankees, so the company was fairly well received. According to the *Virginia Gazette*, they performed "before a numerous and polite audience, with great applause," the audience having been previously assured by the same newspaper that they could expect to be "entertain'd in as polite a manner as in the theatres of London, the company being perfected in all the best plays, operas, farces and pantomimes."[11] They stayed on for a year in Williamsburg, performing with considerable success plays by Shakespeare and some Restoration pieces.

Encouraged by their success in the South, the company decided to try their luck in New York. There, a different reception awaited them. They were not granted permission to perform, even though Lewis Hallam pleaded with the authorities that his people "were not cast in the same mold with our theatrical predecessors; or that in private life or public occupation, we have the least affinity to them,"[12] a statement which only tended to reinforce the prejudices against actors as a profession. Eventually the authorities relented, and the Hallams successfully performed in New York for about half a year. From New York they went to Philadelphia where they were allowed to perform, but only after they publicly announced that they would show nothing indecent or immoral.

After Lewis Hallam died, the management of the company was taken over by the actor David Douglass who also married Hallam's widow. Douglass opened a "histrionic academy" in New York, and announced that he would give dissertations there on moral subjects.

There was trouble everywhere. In Providence an enraged mob threatened to burn down the theatre, and minor acts of violence were the order of the day. We have the record of an announcement Douglass published in which he offered a reward to "whoever can discover the Person who was so rude to throw Eggs from the Gallery, upon the stage last Monday, by which the Cloathes in the Boxes were spoiled, and the Performance in some measure interrupted."[13] Significantly, the reward was a "pistole."

One bright spot in the otherwise dreary story of the Douglass theatre was the regular patronage of George Washington. He kept a box in the company's John Street Theatre in New York, and later at the Chestnut Street Theatre in Philadelphia.

Washington's example, however, did not deter others from condemning the stage again and again. The final blow was a resolution adopted by the Continental Congress on October 20, 1744, banning "cock fighting, exhibition of shews, plays, and other expensive diversions and entertainments." Soon after, the Douglass company left the United States for the friendlier shores of Jamaica.

The Hallam-Douglass company had suffered not only from the hands of its enemies, but from fans as well. The behavior of the friendly audience was abominable; it seems that people went to the theatre not only to see a show but to discharge their aggression. Washington Irving, the leading man of letters of the period who also had the distinction of being one of America's first theatre critics, wrote in one of his feuilletons in the *Morning Chronicle*: "The noise in that part of the house [the gallery] is somewhat similar to that which prevailed in Noah's Ark; for we have an imitation of the whistles and yells of every kind of animal . . . and they commenced a discharge of apples, nuts and gingerbread on the heads of the honest folks in the pit."[14]

As for the actors of his time, Irving's reply to a letter from a fictitious friend shows them to be a pretty shabby lot, leading a hand-to-mouth existence. Irving cautions his friends not to "degenerate" into becoming a critic, "the very pest of society." For what does a critic do if not "rob the actor of his reputation—the public of their amusement," by exposing the faults of the acting and the production. "Hath not an actor eyes, and shall he not wink? If you censure his follies, does he not complain? If you take away his bread, will he not starve? If you starve him, will he not die? And if you kill him, will not his wife and seven small infants, six at her back and one at her breast, rise up and cry vengeance against you?"[15]

Despite public animosity toward the theatre, as the new century dawned there was considerable theatre life in America; a number of buildings were erected especially for the purpose, and already Americans were entering the profession, though it was still English actors who played the leading parts. It was they who brought to America the type of Romantic actor whose private life matched his excesses on the stage; the eccentric, hard drinking, scandalizing actor who aroused passionate admiration, envy, and hatred in his audiences.

The most important of those was, of course, Edmund Kean, England's prime tragedian, whose appearances, initially at least, were received with enthusiasm and riots that threatened the man's very life. Another was George Frederick Cooke whose drinking was so notorious that people went to the theatre in the happy expectation of seeing him fall down during a performance. William Dunlap, the playwright, theatre manager, landscape painter, and first historian of the American theatre, held for a while the thankless job of Cooke's personal manager. He eventually wrote the actor's biography based partially on Cooke's own journals. We read there about a typical day in the life of the actor, spent drinking wine and brandy, until the evening when he was bundled into a hack and delivered into the hands of a dresser while the show was already in progress, the theatre manager in a state of hysteria, and the audience gleefully expecting the unexpected. "He played the first act tolerably but the second was stopped by hisses. He walked up the stage, and was followed by Johnstone, who played Sir Callaghan. After a minute's pause, Johnstone came forward, and addressing the audience in full brogue, said: 'Ladies and Gentlemen—Mr. Cooke says he can't spake.' This laconic apology was received with roars of laughter, and the curtain dropped amidst the most violent tokens of disapprobation levelled at Cooke.''[16]

Another English actor who came to seek his fortune in America was Junius Brutus Booth, Kean's great rival and the founder of the first American theatrical family. True to the pattern, Booth senior was an alcoholic and an intermittent psychotic; of his son Edwin who eventually became America's foremost Shakespearean actor, an admirer wrote that ''All his mistakes and most of his troubles resulted from the amiable weakness with which he sometimes permitted himself to become entangled with paltry, scheming, unworthy people'';[17] as for John Wilkes, as talented as his father and his brother, he is, of course, the most famous of the Booth family as the man who shot president Lincoln.

The performances of English star actors were also the beginning of the celebrity system, a theatre built around one flamboyant performer who drew crowds—with the rest of the actors reduced to the roles of mere supporters on the stage, and to penury and insecurity in life. While actors banded together in earlier times to form a stock company where the profits, meagre as they might have been, were shared in a more or less equitable manner, now it was the star who collected fabulous fees, and on whose continued ability to draw crowds the miserable living of the others depended. ''A Star,'' wrote Stanley Kimmel, a theatre critic of the period, ''is an actor who belongs to no theatre, but travels from each to all, playing a few weeks at a time . . . sustained in his chief character by the regular or stock characters.'' As for the latter, he ''is a good actor and a poor fool. A Star is an advertisement in tights, who grows rich and corrupts public taste.''[18]

The first native-born American star was Edwin Forrest, an actor who aroused wild passions in the audience with his flamboyant acting, and became the standard bearer of theatrical ''nativism,'' a reaction to British imports, to what Walt Whitman called ''cast off dramas, and the unengaged players of Great Britain.''

A man of powerful build, his huge chest and muscles developed by strenuous exercise buttressed by a special diet, Forrest was an awe-inspiring figure on the stage. One of his great roles was Spartacus, the leader of the slave revolt in Rome, in a play *The Gladiators*, a role for which he was eminently suited by his magnificent physique and powerful voice. The highlight of the play was a speech ending with the words "Death to Roman friends, that make their mirth / out of the groans of bleeding misery! / Ho, slaves arise! it is your hour to kill!"[19] Each time he finished the speech the audience leaped to its feet cheering, whereupon the cast froze waiting for the cheering to subside, then Forrest bowed, and the action was resumed. A reporter present at a performance wrote that the excitement was "unsurpassed in any theatre in the world."

Another of Forrest's famous parts was the Indian chief Metamora in a play by the same name, a "noble Indian" who was much the fashion in America of the 1840s. In that role, a critic wrote, his style matching the subject, Forrest's "voice surged and roared like the angry sea; as it reached its boiling, seething climax, in which the serpent hiss of hate was heard, an interval amidst its louder, deeper, hoarser tones, it was like the falls of Niagara, in its tremendous down-sweeping cadence; it was a whirlwind, a tornado, a cataract of illimitable rage."[20]

Forrest skillfully chose parts with an appeal to the sentiments of his audiences: the hatred of tyranny in a nation which had only recently cast off foreign rule, the romanticism of the "noble savage" they had all but exterminated. He also made the most of the fact that he was the first native star. *Metamora*, written by John Augustus Stone, an actor who had frequently played with Forrest and knew well what pleased him, had a prologue asking the audience to judge the "native powers" evident in the play, the author, and the actor.[21]

Carrying the banner of theatrical nationalism, Forrest decided to invade the theatres of England. He was well received there by the audiences which were impressed by the vitality and the sheer physical power of the American. In the play *Damon and Pythias* he lifted one of the characters by his throat and swung him around the stage.

The critics were less enthusiastic, though there were those who found Forrest to be on a par with great English tragedians, including the reigning king of the British stage, William Charles Macready. The latter naturally was not pleased with the comparison, and his displeasure was voiced by John Forster, the theatre critic of the *Examiner* who doubled as Macready's literary adviser. Forster made biting remarks about Forrest's provincial pronunciation, thought that his Richard III looked like "a savage newly caught from out of the American backwoods." In the scene in *Macbeth* where the messenger announces that Birnham Wood was moving, Forrest lifted the hapless fellow from the ground, and threw him across the stage. Forster thought that no English actor, no matter how lowly, deserved to be so manhandled.

Seven years later Macready arrived in the United States for guest appearances, saw Forrest on the stage, and was unimpressed. "He is no artist," Macready wrote in his journal. "Let him be an American actor—and a great American actor—but keep on this side of the Atlantic, and no one will gainsay his comparative excellence."[22]

Forrest thought differently, for in the same year he again went to England, hoping to find there the kind of recognition that would definitely place him in the same class as the great English tragedians. There, the simmering Forrest-Macready hostility burst into a real feud. Forrest claimed that Macready had hired people to hiss at him during his opening performance of *Othello*, which so unnerved him that when he came to the suicide scene he nearly stabbed himself for real. And Forster, still the critic for the *Examiner*, and still Macready's adviser, called his Lear "a roaring pantaloon," though other critics who had been indifferent to Forrest's Othello and Macbeth considered his Lear a triumph.

Forrest retaliated by attending Macready's performance of *Hamlet* in Edinburg, and loudly hissed at him in the scene where the prince of Denmark pretends unconcern before the entry of the players. Macready had invented for that scene a bit of stage business of which he was particularly proud, prancing up and down the stage, waving a handkerchief. When Forrest's hissing became a cause célèbre, the American did not deny that he hissed at the actor, and claimed that he was only exercising the right of a ticket holder to express his displeasure at a piece of acting he found ludicrous.

When several months later Macready again visited the United States, Forrest was determined to make his English rival's tour as difficult as he could; one of the devices was to schedule his own performances, of the same plays, parallel to those of the visitor, the advantage being clearly on his side in view of the nationalistic, anti-British sentiments then prevailing. The result was that emotions flared up and Macready's *Macbeth* in New York was brutally disrupted by rowdies hissing, shouting, and throwing garbage on the stage. The actor somehow managed to get through the performance, and even decided to go on with the next one two evenings later.

It was a courageous but unfortunate decision. On that evening, May 10, 1849, a riot erupted on Astor Place in front of the theatre where Macready was performing. Police, militia, and army detachments had to be called out, and when the fighting ended there were thirty-one dead and many more wounded lying on the pavement. Macready was whisked out of the theatre in a disguise, protected by friends against the rioters who openly proclaimed their intention to kill him. He spent the night at a friend's home while hooligans were ransacking his hotel. In the morning he travelled by coach to New Rochelle where he boarded a train to Boston. The manoeuvre saved his life; a band of hate-crazed men armed with cudgels and knives had broken into that train at the New York station looking for the Englishman. When he arrived in Boston, the mayor and the chief of police went to his hotel to assure him that he would be safe in their city while waiting for the boat to take him back to Britain. He sailed two days later.

Throughout the affair Forrest went about giving his performances, though his audiences had fallen off, possibly because his fans were otherwise occupied, and the day after the riot he wrote a friend a hypocritical, as well as ungrammatical, letter in which he said: "I most sincerely regret to say that last night, the military fired upon the people who were standing outside the Astor House Theatre and many wounded. This blood will rest upon the heads of the Committee who insisted that Mr. Macready should perform in despite of the known wishes of the people to the contrary, and on the heads of the public authorities who were requested by many of the citizens to close the house, and thereby prevent any farther demonstrations."[23]

The Astor Place riot is probably history's most extreme example of the dual emotions—adulation and hatred—generated by actors, those emotions taking on many guises. Here it was the guise of a particularly repulsive form of nationalism, the action taken ostensibly to protect a native actor against the competition of a foreigner.

The finishing touch was provided by the attorney who defended one of the inciters of the riot, a certain E.Z.C. Judson, better known under his pen name Ned Buntline, a hack writer credited with the invention of the dime novel. Mr. Judson only exercised his inalienable American right to free speech and freedom of assembly, the attorney contended. And he added: "Acting is not a concededly useful art, protected by the law, but it is a mode of fashion which depends for its existence upon the gratification for the public in an unrestrained way."[24]

NOTES

1. J. C. Furnas, *The Americans: A Social History of the United States, 1587-1914* (New York: G. P. Putnam & Sons, 1969), p. 564.

2. Ibid.

3. J. S. Buckingham, *America: Historical, Statistic and Descriptive* (London: Fisher & Co., 1940), pp. 47-48.

4. Hugh Rankin, *The Theatre in Colonial America* (Chapel Hill: University of North Carolina Press, 1965), p. 4.

5. Ibid., p. 6.

6. Arthur Hornblow, *A History of the Theatre in America*, vol. 1, *From the Beginning to the Civil War* (New York: Benjamin Bloom, 1919), p. 24.

7. Ibid., p. 102.

8. Ibid., p. 111.

9. John Smith, *Diary of John Smith*, in *History of Theatre in America*, Hornblow, p. 53.

10. Hornblow, *History of Theatre in America*, p. 67.

11. Richard Moody, "American Actors, Managers, Producers and Directors," in *American Drama*, ed. Travis Bogard, Richard Moody, and Walter J. Meserve, vol. 8 of *The Revels History of Drama in English* (London: Barnes and Noble, 1977), p. 81.

12. Ibid.

13. Howard Taubman, *The Making of the American Theatre* (New York: Coward McCann, 1965), p. 37.

14. Quoted in A. M. Nagler, *A Source Book in Theatrical History* (New York: Dover, 1952), p. 525.

15. Taubman, *Making of the American Theatre*, p. 65.

16. William Dunlap, *History of the American Theatre*, vol. 2 (New York: Burt Franklin, 1963), p. 340.

17. William Winter, quoted in Nagler, *Theatrical History*, p. 565.

18. Stanley Kimmel, *The Mad Booths of Maryland* (New York: Bobbs Merrill Co., 1940).

19. Richard Moody, *Edwin Forrest* (New York: Alfred A. Knopf, 1960), p. 102.

20. Ibid., p. 96.

21. Ibid., p. 95.

22. William Charles Macready, *The Diaries of William Charles Macready, 1832-1851*, ed. J. C. Trewin (London: Longmans, Green & Co., 1967), p. 207.

23. Alan S. Downer, *The Eminent Tragedian: William Charles Macready* (Cambridge: Harvard University Press, 1966), p. 309.

24. Ibid.

10

Knights, Courtesans, Matinee Idols

Surely, after all, acting is nonsense.

Sarah Kemble

On July 18, 1895, a date still considered epoch-making in the English theatre, Henry Irving, the country's leading actor, was knighted by Queen Victoria, the first actor to merit such distinction.

The impact of the event, not only in England but throughout the world, seems to our contemporary eyes to have been all out of proportion to its intrinsic meaning. Thousands of cables and letters arrived from all over the world and, on that evening, when Irving appeared on the stage as King Arthur, he was given a standing ovation. On the day following the dubbing, actors from all over England gathered at the Lyceum to present Sir Henry with a congratulatory address signed by more than four thousand members of the profession. The progressive press hailed the event as a victory over puritanism which had always militated against the theatre and the actor. As for the puritans, they had their compensation. On the very same day Irving's knighthood was announced, the judges at the Old Bailey sentenced Oscar Wilde, one of the most successful playwrights of the period, to two years of hard labor for buggery.

Henry Irving was as eminent a Victorian as ever graced the salons of London. A contemporary cartoon shows the Prince of Wales handing him an invitation to dinner at Balmoral Castle, and the actor replying: "The fact is, I am so pestered with invitations to dinner that you really must excuse me!"

He lectured at Oxford and to learned societies, he lived on a lavish though not ostentatious scale, as befitting a man of his standing and income, and he was most conservative in his views. So conservative was he that in his public utterances he always tried to justify his profession on the grounds of its being highly moral. "The main stream of dramatic sentiment," he once said in a lecture, "is pure, kindly, righteous, and, in a sense, religious."[1] He always insisted—at a time when the new naturalist plays by Zola, Ibsen, and Shaw stressed the ugly undersides of contemporary society—that nature ought to be interpreted on the stage "with grace, with dignity, and with temperance."[2]

Henry Irving was born John Brodribb, the son of a fairly prosperous, respectable keeper of a village store. His decision to become an actor was understandably ill received by his parents, especially his pious mother. Laurence Irving, the actor's grandson and official biographer, writes that "Mary Brodribb never found it in her heart to forgive her son: she believed sincerely that inevitably his soul was damned; all that remained was to pray more devoutly than ever that one day he might see the light and that until that time God would protect him from evils and temptations which surely must assail him."[3]

He started out on his acting career against the advice of an actor he admired. "Do not go on the stage," said Samuel Phelps to him. "It is an ill-requited profession." And his wife was reported to remark on their way home after a much-applauded opening: "Are you going to make a fool of yourself like this for the rest of your life?"

Irving completely dominated the theatre life of Britain in the last three decades of the century, a period characterized by the growing respectability of the profession. In 1880, at a public celebration marking Irving's hundreth performance in *The Merchant of Venice*, Lord Houghton stated that the acting profession had acquired the "traditions of good breeding and high conduct," so that "families of condition" should no longer frown on seeing their sons and daughters entering the stage as a career.[4]

With all the progress toward respectability, it is doubtful whether Lord Houghton was expressing the prevailing opinions of the English people. Three months before the historic event at Buckingham Palace, George Bernard Shaw wrote in the *Saturday Review*:

Numbers of respectable English people still regard a visit to the theatre as a sin; and numbers more, including most of those who have become accustomed to meeting even rank-and-file actors and actresses in society where thirty years ago they would have as soon expected to meet an acrobat, would receive a proposal from an actor for the hand of their daughter with a sense of mésalliance which they would certainly not have if the suitor were a lawyer, a doctor, a clergyman or a painter.[5]

One of those parents was Charles Dickens, a lover and a staunch supporter of the theatre. About forty years after he wrote the article in the *Saturday Review,* Shaw recalled in a speech delivered to students of drama how the novelist reacted when his own daughter announced her intention to become an actress: "You would not expect Charles Dickens to have any prejudice against the theatre of the ordinary kind, of the kind of parent who imagines that the theatre is the gate to hell. And yet when his daughter wanted to go on the stage . . . he absolutely refused to allow her to think of such a thing. . . . The theatre was a place into which his daughter could not go in a professional capacity."[6]

Had Shaw carefully read Dickens's kindly description of the lives and characters of actors in *Nicholas Nickleby,* he would have not been surprised by the novelist's horror at his daughter's plans. With all his love for the theatre, Dickens saw actors of his time as not far removed from the vagabonds of a generation earlier; he looked upon strolling mummers as closely related to gypsies, tinkers, and peddlers.

The theatre in late Victorian England was at a state of unprecedented bloom, in quantity that is. The Industrial Revolution caused a massive resettlement from the country to the city where workers led bleak lives of dawn-to-dusk labor, their drudgery no longer relieved by the seasonal and family celebrations which had once formed part of their traditional way of life. This created a thirst for entertainment. "People mutht be amused," says Sleary of *Hard Times*: "They can't be alwayth working nor yet they can't be alwayth learning." A contemporary observer having attended a performance at the Sadler Wells, wrote more piously than accurately that "there sit our working classes in a happy crowd, as orderly and reverent as if they were at church."[7]

Following the abolition of the patent system in 1843, theatres proliferated at an alarming rate in London and in the provinces, ranging from the ultrarespectable establishments in London's West End to the utterly disreputable "gaffs" where the actors had to make themselves heard over the noise of drunken customers, from Shakespeare and the fashionable contemporary comedies to the melodramas where murder and mayhem reigned supreme.

The conservative elements in society led by the church believed that the theatre was an inherently immoral institution, but since it had proven impossible to stem the rising tide, they fell back on strict censorship in order to lessen the evil. Clergymen preached that sordid acts seen on the stage, such as murder and seduction, actually led the viewers to imitate them in life. Melodrama was immoral and so was Shakespeare with all the gore in his plays, with acts and utterances which went against the teachings of religion, against the principles of modesty and morality. Strict censorship of plays was instituted in order to eliminate the most blatant manifestations of theatre's immorality.

The acting community, or at least the upper layer of the profession, responded to those pressures by a concerted effort to improve its image in the eyes of the people, to present themselves to the public as law-abiding, God-fearing citizens who earn their living by hard toil. Anxious to comply with the censor, they picked "safe" plays, and even those plays were disembarrassed of sexual references and of references to religion and the clergy. This was often carried to ridiculous lengths; in the play *A Clerical Error*, the phrase "Neither on earth nor in heaven" was deleted.[8]

The magazine *Theatre* took upon itself the task of turning actors into respectable citizens, teaching them to behave properly both on and off stage. The magazine's editorials maintained that only the most responsible man could be a good actor, and only a pure woman could properly tread the stage.

The leading personalities in the profession spared no effort to present themselves to the public as proper Victorian ladies and gentlemen. George Alexander who managed the ultrarespectable St. James Theatre Company was strolling one morning on Bond Street attired in Prince Albert coat, silk hat, and gloves when he met two members of his company. The young man was wearing a soft hat and a tweed suit, and the girl sported similarly casual dress.

Alexander politely responded to their greeting, expressed his satis-faction at seeing two members of the company on friendly terms, then proceeded to berate them for not living up to the social obliga-tions in dress as behooved members of the company.

It was the same George Alexander who on the day Oscar Wilde was sentenced deleted the name of the author from the billboard of the successfully running *The Importance of Being Earnest.*

The drive to improve the reputation of the profession extended even more so to actresses. The popular image of the actress as being a somewhat better class of whore took a long time dying, the per-sistence of this image aided by the fact that in some theatres this was not far from the truth. As late as at the turn of the century Shaw described some variety theatres in the provinces as being "a drink shop and a prostitution market," where the girls were picked not for their acting skill but for their price on the flesh market. It was also customary for whores when they were picked up by the police to give their occupation as actress, many of them having at one time or another appeared on the stage.

In a society that assigned to women the strictly limited role of dutiful wife whose proper place was at home caring for her hus-band and children, where only women of the lowest social class went to work in factories or as domestics—the other most common way to earn a living being prostitution—the actress occupied a place somewhere in between. Apart from the perennial stigma attaching to the acting profession, the Victorian actress was pretty close to the social bottom simply as a working woman, in addition to being a woman who violated the prevailing principles of modesty by displaying herself publicly. "Doesn't one have to be a strange girl," wrote proper Victorian Henry James, "to want to go and exhibit one's self to a loathsome crowd, on a platform, with trum-pets and a big drum, for money—to parade one's body and one's soul?"[9]

On the brighter side, an actress's rewards were considerable, if she was successful. Hers was the only profession where she was on equal terms with men, in working conditions and earnings. And she had the extra advantage, if she was endowed with good looks, of being able to advance on the strength of her looks alone.

Not only the advertisements but the critics also stressed the sexual attractiveness of female performers. John Elsom in his

Erotic Theatre quotes some of the overtly sexual phrases used in the press to describe an actress, such as "the barmaid who only gives the public what they want," or "a romp, a delicious hoyden," or "a joyous creature abounding in life." Even so august a stage personality as Ellen Terry had been praised for her "winsome womanliness."[10] George Bernard Shaw called his fellow critics a band of voluptuaries.

Actresses who had reached the top of the profession were anxious to exclude themselves from that raffish, sexual image. They chose parts calling for dignity in behavior and dress. Margaret Kendal went as far as to refuse to play Shakespeare whom she found not quite respectable.

The growing respectability of the profession inevitably had its detrimental effect on the British theatre of the day. Not only did it affect the repertory by eliminating plays liable to offend public mores—which meant most plays of any merit—but acting was becoming sterile as performers, especially female, feared to display true emotions, lest they become suspect of having led a nonsheltered life. In an age when people believed with William Acton (*Treaties on the Functions and Disorders of the Reproductive Organs*) that only loose and vulgar women enjoy sex, while women of morals and refinement know no such base sensations, how could an actress allow herself to portray a woman in the throes of passion? George Bernard Shaw realized this when he wrote that the range of an actress's performance calls for the kind of knowledge and experience in life which is forbidden to "pure" women.

As the century was nearing its end, actors and actresses and the theatre, especially in London's West End, became genteel on both sides of the proscenium. The audience came mainly from the affluent circles, and acquired the habit of evening dress and early dining before going to the theatre to listen to the chitchat of well-bred actors.

This new breed of actors carried over to the twentieth century. Somerset Maugham, a successful playwright in the twenties, complained that actors were no longer the fascinating people they used to be: "The actors have become settled, respectable and well-to-do. It offended them to be thought a race apart and they have done their best to be like everybody else. They have shown themselves to us without their make-up in the broad light of day, and besought us to see for ourselves that they are golfers and taxpayers and thinking men and women. To my mind this is all stuff and nonsense.''[11]

The actors of whom Somerset Maugham wrote, and the actors who preceded them by a generation, constituted only part, and a small one, too, of the profession. Irving's knighthood by no means meant that the profession had finally "arrived," that actors had become "gentlemen," in the contemporary sense of the word. "If we grant that the representative of the Prince of Denmark is well entitled to rank as gentleman or even to receive the dignity of knighthood," a critic asked, "are we quite sure about the personator of the Second Gravedigger?''[12]

The Second Gravedigger had little share in the prosperity and the newly won respectability of the profession, especially if he worked outside of London. The field was overcrowded, and competition was fierce leading to exploitation by managers who saw in the theatre a source of quick profits. When the expected profits did not materialize and the venture failed, it was the actor who paid for it, in terms of salaries never received. And if he dared to sue, he would be blacklisted and never have a chance to work again.

Around the end of the century actors in England could be roughly divided into three categories: stars, resident members of established companies, and the large gray mass of actors of various degrees of talent and skill with no regular employment. While the first usually earned huge sums, those immediately below them had to contend themselves with modest remunerations, and the third category led a precarious existence, much of the time unemployed, earning a bare subsistence. They frequently had to subsidize the management by supplying their own costumes, wigs, and even props, and were forced to function as the management's publicity agents by distributing leaflets throughout town.

The reception given to strolling actors in the provinces varied; the population in most places was friendly, the authorities were frequently hostile. Edward Stirling, a strolling actor, manager, and hack playwright, recalls in his memoirs how he went to the town of Romford in Essex where he applied at the local magistrate for permission to perform. His "humble request" was met with the following reaction: "What sir! bring your beggarly actors into this town to demoralize the people? No sir! I'll have no such profligacy in Romford; poor people shall not be wheedled out of their money by your tomfooleries. The First player that comes here I'll clap him in stocks as a rogue and a vagabond. Good-morning, sir."[13]

Also, the physical working conditions added to the misery of the actor. Even the fine London theatres with their ornate halls had dingy, poorly lit, and badly ventilated and heated dressing rooms. Conseqently consumption and pulmonary diseases were quite frequent in the profession, and many actors died of them. The chief aim of the Actors' Association, established in 1891, was to have management improve conditions backstage. It ought to be noted that the reformers of the period, the fighters for better conditions for the working class and for women's rights, paid little attention to actors. When they did, it was to moralize them rather than to see that they earned a decent living under reasonable working conditions.

At the bottom of the profession were actors employed in the "gaffs" which catered to the poorest of audiences. In the late 1850s it was estimated that London had one hundred such establishments. Some of the actors employed had known better days, but most of them were men and women who drifted into the profession, and despite the wretchedness it brought them clung to it because they could see no other way to live. So dismal was their condition that often quarrels broke out over who should eat the stage food. One of those actors wrote out of his bitterness: "Who but one haunted by a restless burning desire for dramatic distinction would welcome years of poverty, privation, sickness of soul and body, a constant sense of self-imposed beggary, and an internal reproach for frequent acts of meanness not to be avoided, and even dishonesty, which may not be shunned."[14] One recalls the "host of shabby, poverty stricken men" of the *Pickwick Papers* who regularly hung around the theatres hoping for a bit part.

While the second part of the nineteenth century in England was fully dominated by the person of the plain, prudish, Protestant-bourgeois Queen Victoria, across the channel *la vie Parisienne* was in full bloom, with its excessive love of luxury, its extravagant display of wealth, its mad pursuit of pleasure—all of it presided over by Emperor Napoleon III and Empress Eugénie.

The *tout le monde* of the Second Empire lived as if the French Revolution of a century ago had never taken place; the new aristocracy and the *nouveau riche* wallowed in their wealth, the lady most apt to be admired being one who invented a new way to spend money. One of them was Princess Metternich who was known due to her singular homeliness as the best dressed monkey in Paris. She once walked into her loge at the Comédie Française in a dress all strewn with diamonds, preceded by two liveried footmen, each of them carrying a huge candelabrum.

One of the social phenomena of the period was the small but highly visible class called *demi-monde*, a term given currency by Alexander Dumas fils whose play by that title was one of the sensations of the Parisian theatre in 1855. It was a class of women who, in Dumas's words, inhabited that shadowy space where the legal wife ended and the mistress began. In *Le Demi-monde* one character explains to another: "It is neither the aristocracy nor the bourgeoisie, but it floats on the ocean of Paris, and it summons, gathers in, and admits all those who fail or emigrate or escape from one of those continents—as well as the chance victims of shipwrecks, who come from none knows where." How does one recognize the *demi-mondaine*? "By the absence of a husband."[15]

The Paris theatre of the Second Empire was inextricably bound with the demi-monde; in a strange intertwining, the demi-monde was both a frequent subject of plays and the class to which actresses who played in them belonged. The demi-mondaines were the stars, while the lesser practitioners of the profession, from the run-of-the-mill actresses to performers in the cheapest places, were associated—at least in the eyes of the public—with prostitution in its various forms. Never before, or after, in the Western world was the theatre so closely associated with sexual licence and commercial sex.

The French theatre in the second part of the century moved from Romantisicm to realism, from the idealized heroic past to the day-to-day not at all heroic present. The bourgeoisie which formed the bulk of the theatre audience were people leading down-to-earth existences. Unlike the aristocracy of the ancien régime with their artificial lives and manner of thinking, they looked at life through realistic eyes and, secure in their newly won dominant position in society, were not even afraid of criticism.

One of the exponents of the new realism was Alexander Dumas fils whose *La dame aux camélias* is the most characteristic, in addition to having been one of the most successful, plays of the period.

Dumas based the plot on the real-life story of Marie Duplessis, one of the *grande cocottes* of his time who died young to be mourned by her poet and artist friends, while her upper-class admirers were conspicuously absent at her funeral. The play purported to be a condemnation of high bourgeois society and high bourgeois morals. Marguerite Gauthier, the heroine, was sincerely in love with Armand, and ready to give up her lucrative way of life for the sake of this love, but the romance and Marguerite were destroyed by Armand's wealthy, influential father, a representative of his class.

Seen through our contemporary eyes, the play is little more than a sentimental tearjerker, culminating in the famous scene of Marguerite's dying. Also, a cocotte as the embodiment of pure love makes for a rather specious argument, but *La dame aux camélias* depicted with great accuracy both the demi-monde and the monde and, despite its fashionable character, was a moralistic tale, a forerunner of the plays of the "naturalists."

It was both a popular success and a *succès de scandale*. A contemporary chronicler wrote that "this play is shameful for the epoch which allows it, the government which tolerates it, the public which applauds it . . . it is in fact a full-scale public outrage."[16]

It is perhaps due to the storm of protests the play provoked that Dumas followed it with another, on the same subject but with a different approach. *Le demi-monde* had the tables turned; the whore no longer had a heart of gold, and the marriage between a young man "of good family" and a demi-mondaine ended in disaster.

With all its shallowness and artificiality, the character of Marguerite was a great vehicle for many actresses. Of those none was greater than Sarah Bernhardt. Bernhardt epitomized not only the theatre but the period in which she lived. Of illegitimate birth, the daughter of a Jewish-Dutch mother and a French father, she was born into the demi-monde; her mother and her aunt all led the gay, glamorous lives of successful courtesans. By the time Sarah was fifteen, her mother had reached the pinnacle of her profession, having acquired as a lover the immensely rich Duc de Morny. According to the actress's biographers, it was the duke who suggested that the girl be sent to the Conservatoire to study acting, so as to get rid of a troublesome youngster.

Throughout her fabulously successful career, which lasted an incredible sixty years, Sarah Bernhardt lived the life of a demimondaine par excellence. She never married, but had a son fathered by one of her innumerable lovers, reputedly a Danish prince. Her friendly biographers stress that none of her liaisons were made for the purpose of gain, material or other, and that she was particularly attracted to very handsome men, which is the reason why they discount the rumors of her romance with François Sarcey who was the most influential theatre critic of the day but an extremely homely man.

It was not at all necessary for an actress to be endowed with Sarah Bernhardt's extraordinary talent to achieve fame and riches. Cora Pearl, a minor performer in comic operas—according to Joanna Richardson, a historian of the Second Empire—was

> so rich that her jewels alone were worth a million francs, she had two or three houses furnished quite regardless of expense, and she showed the lavishness of all the grand cocottes, choosing some of her clothes at Worth's, giving stupendous entertainment, grand dinners, masked balls and impromptu suppers. . . . Early in 1866 she appeared as Eve at a fancy dress ball at the Restaurant des Trois Fréres Provenceaux. She looked very well, reported an English journalist, "and her form and figure were not concealed by any more garments than were worn by the original apple-eater."[17]

The Franco-Prussian War of 1870, the fall of the Second Empire, then the Paris Commune put an end to the gay party. In the words of Emile Zola, it was the end "of a dead reign, of a strange epoch of folly and shame." The wealthy were still wealthy, but ostentatious display of wealth was no longer the fashion, and the days of the *grande cocotte* displaying herself on the stage were over.

Simultaneously a new kind of theatre arose in Paris, a theatre showing plays where the action did not take place in salons decorated in white and gold, but in middle class homes and in slums. André Antoine, an amateur actor who earned his living as a clerk at the gas company, founded the Théâtre Libre to perform the works of Zola, Ibsen, and Hauptmann; plays exposing the corruption of bourgeois society. The realism of Dumas gave way to the naturalism of Zola, the sentimental, wronged Marguerite was replaced by the brutal Nana who used her beautiful body as an instrument of revenge on the corrupt and corruptible rich. The good citizens of Paris and the provinces were horrified at the immorality of the theatre which dared to show such ugly aspects of life, and began to shun the theatre lest their morals be impaired.

A similar phenomenon appeared in other countries of the West where equivalents of the Théâtre Libre sprang up to come to grips with the real problems of life. There was the Freie Buehne in Germany, the Independent Theatre in England, the Irish Literary Theatre, the Art Theatre of Stanislavski and Nemirovich-Danchenko in Russia. The theatre which over many decades served mainly as the provider of thrills for the masses and mild entertainment for the well to do, reawakened to its real role in society—which again made it morally suspect. Ibsen and Zola were banned or were performed over the objections of the church and lay authorities, and the men and women who acted in those plays were the chief culprits.

In America, a late-comer to the theatrical scene, the second part of the nineteenth century amounted to a veritable theatrical explosion. The rapidly growing population and the growing wealth created a huge demand for entertainment of every kind, and the more conservative elements of society, especially the church, could no longer stem the tide. Hundreds of strolling companies were criss-crossing the vastness of the country, their members by now being mostly native born, and with little if any training. The male actors imitated Edwin Forrest, America's first native-born stage star. They were robust men with iron lungs who greatly appealed to the rowdies in the galleries. Amazingly enough, the female stars matched their partners in size and lung power. The most famous of them, Charlotte Cushman, a woman of Amazonian size with square shoulders, generous hips and bosom, with a husky voice which could fill the largest hall, was a famous Lady Macbeth, and also played Hamlet and Romeo.

The star system ruled unchecked; a theatrical company was little more than a group of men and women hired to support the star, and it hardly mattered whether they knew anything about acting because so little attention was paid to them. As for the other stars, some of them became a success in a single part, then spent the rest of their professional lives playing that part. The most famous of those actors—having been immortalized in the plays of his son—was James O'Neill. A capable actor on his way to becoming a good all-around performer, he had the misfortune of scoring a hit as the Count of Monte Cristo in a dramatization of the novel by Dumas *père*, and from then on did nothing but swashbuckle his way through American theatres, amassing a fortune in the process.

In the last quarter of the century the star system gave birth to the matinee idol, and much of the history of the American theatre for about half a century or so hence revolves around that phenomenon.

It seems that the term *matinee*, meaning literally a morning performance, was first used by Thackeray who refers in *Vanity Fair* to a "matinee musical." Due to a strange evolution to which words are prone, especially when crossing an ocean, the term began around the 1870s to signify a performance taking place in the afternoon, a performance attended almost exclusively by ladies who had little else to do in the day, and a matinee idol was thus an actor who by virtue of his looks and personality had a special appeal to the female sex.

Stage idolatry is, of course, an ancient phenomenon, with a tradition as old as the Roman theatre when women went demonstratively wild over handsome mimes, the idol being a source of sexual magic, the embodiment of dreams which cannot be satisfied in reality by husbands and lovers.

The matinees were patronized by women who would never have ventured out of the house alone in the evening, lest their reputation be soiled. Moreover, when the lady went to the theatre in the evening, properly chaperoned by husband or parents, she had to maintain a demure stance, while at the matinee, surrounded by other women, she could give vent to her desire to shout, blow kisses, even swoon at the sight of her idol making love to the lucky woman on the stage.

According to William Brady, a famous impressario of the period, the first American matinee idol was Harry Montague. "Matinee audiences couldn't get enough of him. His mail was like a movie star's today. Hundreds of woman used to collect at the stage door every day to watch Harry come and get out of his carriage. . . ."[18]

Montague died young, at the height of his popularity, the victim of a ruptured lung. When the news of his death was announced, thousands of women throughout America exploded in a frenzy of mourning. They walked around with black ribbons across their chests, held weeping demonstrations in front of the theatre where he had appeared, and built huge altars of flowers with the initials H. M. in red carnations.

Another matinee idol was Kyrle Bellew, a Shakespearean actor from London who in 1895 came to America to make his fortune, and much to his dismay found himself a matinee idol, hysterically pursued by women wherever he went. His greatest success was in something called *The Gentleman of France*, where standing on a curved staircase, wearing lacey linen, red tights, and black patent-leather shoes, he ran his sword through four marquises, four viscounts, and six lesser characters, whereupon he embraced a beautiful marchioness as the curtain slowly descended. Three years after his arrival, when tired of all this hokum and having made his bundle Bellew sailed for England, the docks were crammed with screaming, weeping women of all ages; two of them tried to stow away on the ship, and one jumped into the water but was fished out.

There was no female equivalent to the matinee idol; the stage ladies were only mildly popular—if only because men did not attend matinees. However, toward the end of the century the American theatre lost some of the inhibitions regarding the female form, and men flocked there to see a display of legs, and other parts of the body, which in those days were never seen in public— off stage.

An actress by the name of Ada Isaacs Menken, for example, aped in Byron's *Mazeppa* where she dashed across the stage on horseback wearing flesh-colored tights, and a musical extravaganza called *The Black Crook* featured row after row of beautiful girls with a dazzling display of legs and cleavage. George Templeton Strong, a socialite and diarist of the period, called this kind of theatre the "Feminine-femoral school of dramatic art," and observed that the theatre was packed with "men mostly."[19] J. C. Furnas, the historian of American morals, relates that "Strong's wife, a perfect lady of impeccable social standing, made up a party of equally impeccable friends, of both sexes, to go see the show and come home to supper afterwards." The event took place in the late 1880s, the gilded age of prosperity following the Civil War. Remarks Furnas: "Her mother would have died first."[20]

NOTES

1. Michael Baker, *The Rise of the Victorian Actor* (London: Rowman, Littlefield, 1978), p. 60.

2. Ibid.

3. Laurence Irving, *Henry Irving: The Actor and His World* (London: Faber & Faber, 1951), p. 64.

4. Baker, *Rise of the Victorian Actor*, pp. 89-90.

5. George Bernard Shaw, *Saturday Review*, 19 February 1895.

6. George Bernard Shaw, *Shaw on Theatre*, ed. E. J. West (New York: Hill & Wang, 1958), p. 188.

7. Baker, *Rise of the Victorian Actor*, p. 45.

8. Ibid., p. 55.

9. Ibid., p. 95.

10. John Elsom, *The Erotic Theatre* (London: Secker & Warburg, 1973), p. 27.

11. Somerset Maugham, *The Summing Up* (London: William Heinemann, 1948), p. 107.

12. Baker, *Rise of the Victorian Actor*, p. 161.

13. J. C. Trewin, ed., *Theatre Bedside Book: An Anthology of the Stage* (Newton Abbott, Eng.: David & Charles, 1974), p. 168.

14. Baker, *Rise of the Victorian Actor*, p. 131.

15. Joanna Richardson, *La Vie Parisienne* (New York: Viking Press, 1971), p. 137.

16. Ibid., p. 136.

17. Joanna Richardson, *The Courtesans: The Demi-Monde in Nineteenth-Century France* (London: Weidenfeld & Nicolson, 1967).

18. David Carroll, *The Matinee Idols* (London: Peter Owen, 1972), p. 38.

19. J. C. Furnas, *The Americans: A Social History of the United States, 1587-1914* (New York: G. P. Putnam & Sons, 1964), p. 758.

20. Ibid.

11

Salaries and Sex Symbols

> The actor is the only human being who will work for nothing, if you let him.
>
> An official of American Equity

In the second half of the twentieth century the actor was no longer a pariah under the law and custom; he had climbed up from the lowest depths to a position where his profession was widely recognized and admired, and those who reached the top were showered with money and honours. There was glitter and glamour in being an actor—especially in films and television where the rewards, in money and fame, were considerably greater than in the theatre— and no other individual, including political and military leaders, was given more attention in the press or other media.

All of which was sham. The recognition and the riches were the rewards of the very few, of that paper-thin upper stratum of the profession, men and women whose names were household words, while directly below them there writhed a mass of the most insecure, most underpaid, frequently maligned, highly trained professionals reduced to a constant search for work, forced to take on jobs they detested, desperately clinging to a profession which repaid them with cruel disregard for their devotion.

In May 1978, at a national theatre conference in Canada, the president of the Canadian Actors' Equity Association reported: "As for the unemployment situation of the theatre artist in Canada, we're the envy of the western world. Despite all the things you hear about Canada, it is a great place to work. We love it. . . .

In general, our employment record is fantastic. We have, at times, almost 50 percent of our members working."[1]

Such a statement would have sounded like a bad joke, had the speaker been an official of a union of steel workers, truckers, journalists, or accountants. It was not so coming from the mouth of the president of Equity. Unemployment was the chief factor in the professional life of an actor in the Western world, acting was at the bottom as a means of earning a living, especially if one averaged the actor's annual income. According to the above cheerful report, the average income of an Equity member in 1977 was $5,000, considerably below the earnings of a day laborer.

In 1973, London Transport advertised for bus conductors at £34 per week plus various fringe benefits, and the response was disappointing. At the same time lines formed in front of the offices of a theatrical production company when it was learned by the grapevine that they were casting for a new musical. The minimum pay in London's West End was then £20 per week, and there was, of course, no security in a job; some productions closed only a few days after they opened.

In the United States, things looked even worse. In 1975, the executive secretary of American Equity testified before a government committee dealing with subsidies to the theatres. "By and large," he stated, "our people are unemployed or underemployed. And, when they are employed, very poorly paid. It is a little-known fact, but members of our union suffer a 75 to 80 percent unemployment rate. And over 75 percent of our members earn less than $5,000 a year at their profession. Only 5 percent earn more than $10,000 per year."[2]

And if this was not sufficient to destroy the myth about actors earning huge amounts of money—a myth established by newspaper reports about the fabulous way of life of superstars—he further informed the committee that the median income of an actor was about $6,000, and that only one fourth of them were employed a full year. The sum of $6,000 was $1,748 less than the salaries of bus drivers, and considerably less than half of the $14,291 annual salary of a dental hygienist. The average of $6,000 was also $3,200 short of the income which, according to the U.S. Labor Department, was necessary for an urban family to exist on a very low level.

It certainly paid better to move scenery around than to act. In 1972, at the John F. Kennedy Center for the Performing Arts in Washington, actors were paid a respectable $175 per week, while stagehands were earning $1,500.

The situation was slightly better in Western Europe. In the spring of 1977, American reporter Jennifer Merin interviewed François Dunoyer, a fairly successful thirty-year-old actor, in Paris. To the question how did he survive, he replied: "Sometimes I wonder myself. . . . I work on the legitimate stage as often as I can but stage work doesn't always pay so well. So I do a lot of film and television. I guess that you can say that I act wherever and whenever I can."

Asked whether many French actors make a living at their art, he had this to say: "I don't think so. I don't have all the figures but I know that there are more actors than jobs. That's for sure. And there seems to be more actors appearing in Paris every year looking for work." He estimated that there were about ten thousand professional actors in France of which eight thousand lived in Paris, and of those only about one thousand were employed in their profession.[3]

A similar situation prevailed in Italy. In the same series of interviews, a young up-and-coming actress named Patrizia Sacchi was asked whether she earned her entire income from theatre work. "Yes," she replied, "but it is extremely difficult. I only work about seven months a year. That's been the average since I left theatre school. In the months when I'm not working I devote almost all my time and energy to looking for work and I wind up using all of the salary I've saved."[4]

In Denmark, a welfare state par excellence, the actor's lot was considerably better. In 1979 unemployment ran there at about 30 percent, and actors out of work were receiving compensation of 6,500 Kr., approximately $1,300 per month. The minimum salary was 8,000 Kr. in the provinces and 6,000 Kr. in Copenhagen (in consideration of the fact that while working in the capital the actor could pick up extra money in films, television, and so on), while the average salary was about 12,000 Kr., equalling the earnings of a medium-rank civil servant or teacher.

One of the members of the profession who did much to establish the myth of the fabulous income of actors confessed that all through her professional life, she suffered from insecurity so that, in her own words, she never knew where her next magnum of champagne was coming from. Writing in her autobiography, Tallulah Bankhead thus described the actor's lot:

> If he is familiar with elementary economics, the actor must know that even by coolie standards he's doomed, at best, to a lifetime of insecurity, at worst, to slow starvation. Me? I'm an exception. After thirty-three years in the theatre I'm almost even. Shortly I hope to have my Cadillac paid for. With any luck I'll square accounts with the Revenue Bureau next season. I've just received reminders of a few loose and annoying arrears.[5]

There is a steep drop from the earnings of performers whose names are known to the public to the point of having sensational appeal to merely well-known actors. One of the latter, the Broadway actress Marian Seldes, played in Peter Shaffer's *Equus* opposite Richard Burton. The latter was being paid $10,000 a week, while her salary was a mere fraction of that sum. When she asked him whether he intended to do more plays, he replied in the negative—he claimed he could not live on that kind of money (he was at that time married to Elizabeth Taylor).[6]

Actors in the class of Marian Seldes are reasonably well paid when they are working, but unemployment, occasional or permanent, is a constant hazard. A standard character in modern fiction dealing with life in the theatre or movies, is an actress, still young, still attractive, undergoing the daily humiliation of futile job applications, pathetically maintaining her dignity with a false front which does not fool anyone. In one of those novels, an actress shows up in a producer's office, having heard that he was casting for a new picture. The narrator witnessing the scene is a ludicrously overpaid, Richard Burton-type of star: "When the woman came in I recognized her. I'd seen her with Richardson and Olivier at the Old Vic at the end of the war. She had that glazed look that actors get when they have to look for work instead of work looking for them. Goodness knows how many auditions she'd been to in her time. I saw her switch herself on as she came through the door." After a polite charade, the meeting ends on a don't-call-me-I'll-call-you note.[7]

While in most professions—in law, teaching, the sciences—overcrowding or a decreased demand usually cause a drop in school enrollment; the opposite seems to be taking place in the theatre. Since 1904, when the Royal Academy of Dramatic Arts was founded, drama schools in England have proliferated at an alarming rate, spewing out each year thousands of young men and women eager to enter the profession for which they had studied three to four years, knowing that only few of them will succeed, while the rest are condemned to a life of poverty and indignity, of a daily struggle for the crumbs.

In a 1972 letter to the London *Times*, the president of English Equity reported that about one thousand graduate from drama schools each year; in the year 1970/71, 1,428 new members joined Equity. During that year a questionnaire circulated by Equity among its membership revealed that the average amount of work for an actor per year was 14½ weeks in the theatre, and 21 days in films and television; for an actress there were 11½ weeks in the theatre and 7½ days in films and television. In 1972, Equity statisticians estimated that there was enough work in England to provide 6,500 actors and actresses with a reasonable living. The organization's membership at the time stood at about 20,000. At the same time all reputable drama schools had many more candidates for admission than places. At the London Academy of Music and Dramatic Art, 750 candidates competed for 24 places.

Naturally, the actors' earnings are subject to the law of supply and demand, this despite the union's efforts to assure its members of a living wage. In 1966 an experienced actor was earning less than an apprentice coal miner, and when the theatre budget of the Arts Council was practically doubled, the increase was used to cover increased production costs, while actors' salaries remained virtually unchanged.[8]

"The actor is the only human being who will work for nothing, if you let him," said an official of American Equity. He might have added that an actor would even *pay* to be allowed to act—if he had the money. Ralph Richardson started his career in the theatre by paying ten shillings to a man who ran a small, half-amateur, half-professional troupe, performing in what used to be a bacon factory in a London suburb. The arrangement called for Richardson to pay for twenty weeks, and after that the entrepreneur was to pay him.

Needless to say, it was the entrepreneur who gained in the deal, though it was a profitable investment for the actor, in view of the fees Sir Ralph commanded later on.

The picture is quite different in the Soviet Union and other Communist countries where—in a manner reminiscent of his role in ancient Greece—the actor has become part of the state religious observance, playing a vital role in the permanent popular indoctrination process. Actors are officials of the state, with all the advantages and disadvantages of that status. And the advantages are considerable, including thorough training, full employment and job security, as well as financial rewards which place actors on par with the elite of bureaucracy and technocracy.

Actors also enjoy high social status which manifests itself in ranks, medals, and titles which are awarded to all faithful servants of the state. The titles Honored Artist of the USSR and People's Artist of the USSR carry considerable advantages, such as money grants, the right to shop in cooperative stores reserved for the elite, even such minor, but in the Soviet reality important, privileges as the right to board a taxi ahead of the queue. The titles are frequently awarded on the strength of the portrayal of one character, usually a positive one, a hero of labor who overcomes a crisis in the *kolkhoz* (the Soviet collective farm) or unmasks a saboteur.

Occasionally, unexpected factors intervene. When Stalin saw the movie *Chapayev* and expressed his satisfaction at the manner in which the Civil War was portrayed there, the entire huge cast, including the extras playing soldiers and peasants who were recruited from the *kolkhoz*es, were awarded the title Honored Artist of the USSR. Most of those so honored never again appeared in a film. A Moscow theatrical joke has it that Soviet actors can be divided into the following categories: Deserving Honored Artists, Undeserving Honored Artists, Deserving Unhonored Artists, and Undeserving Unhonored Artists.

The situation is similar in other Communist countries, though not all of them practice that Byzantine custom of awarding titles. In Rumania there is no unemployment problem as the authorities keep the number of drama school students down to the estimated number of actors needed. A Rumanian actor told an interviewer that when he applied for admission to the State Theatre Institute, he was one of 1,800 candidates competing for 32 places. Once accepted, he went through a rigorous four-year training program, upon graduation was given a job, and has worked steadily since. His starting salary was a generous 2,000 Lei a month (around $480 according to the official exchange), with regular increases, plus bonuses for special work, as well as automatic increases as the actor's family grew. In fact, actors have contracts for life; openings are created by retirements and deaths.[9]

An American observer, conditions prevailing on Broadway fresh in his mind, was carried away by enthusiasm when he learned how well actors were being treated in the USSR. "Except for the army and the scientists, no citizens are more respected than the artists," wrote Faubion Bowers. "The profession of working in the theatre carries with it dignity and distinction . . . prizes have been lavished on them with regal abundance. A student is guaranteed a job for life, and when he grows tired, pensioned retirement is his if he wants it. Every actor knows that he will always be appearing somewhere in some role with regularity. The nightmare of the out-of-work actor does not exist."

One pays a price, however, for living in that paradise. "Censorship has been technically abolished and scripts no longer have to be submitted to the government agencies," we learn. And the reason for this is simple. As a director friend explained to a writer: "By now all of us know what should or should not be done. If we do plays which strike you as propaganda, it is because we feel that way."[10]

Back in the Western world, the unavoidable question arises why actors are ready to put up with the penury, the insecurity, the indignities imposed on them by the profession. Without going into psychological and sociological investigation, Tallulah Bankhead spelled it out clearly in her own inimitable style: "To put the most charitable construction upon our mass lunacy, it's because we thrive on applause, even random applause. We're harmless megalomaniacs, fanatic in our devotion to a profession which rarely rewards us with a livelihood. Since we court public display, we're the foes of privacy. The glass house is our favorite residence."[11]

Actors, of course, have always lived in glass houses, by the very fact of appearing nightly on the stage, in the flesh, offering their bodies to the public. It has become much more so since the development of the mass media and the discovery that actors make good reading material. Nowadays the public is daily informed about the star's current activities, starting with his or her love life and ending with trivia (there is a book of interviews with movie actors entitled *Do You Sleep in the Nude?*). In the case of movie actors the glass house is one of the most valuable properties of the actor and the studio; a huge publicity industry has been built to manufacture them.

The emergence of the movie actor in the second decade of the century wrought a radical change in the social position of the actor. For one thing, the actor's audience expanded to become virtually unlimited in global terms; instead of the mere thousands who could see an actor in one production on the stage, uncounted millions across geographic, linguistic, and time barriers can see him in a film. For another, the actor of flesh and blood performing only a short distance from the spectator's seat was replaced by a moving shadow while, paradoxically, the close-up brought the actor much closer to the spectator than it had ever been possible on the stage, and thus a more intimate contact was established.

The movies also brought the celebrity system to an extreme never dreamt of in the theatre, the star's popularity bolstered by powerful publicity machines which are as important to the industry as the film production itself. As for the art of acting, it was largely replaced by the projection of the star's personality—in fact a denial of the actor's art which is essentially the ability to assume different personalities.

Then there are the huge sums of money earned by movie actors, incomes far exceeding the earnings of even the most successsful stage actors. As early as 1928, George Bernard Shaw complained about this phenomenon which "never existed in the annals of public life before, and that persons who have not yet grown up [are] becoming possessed of enormous fortunes."[12]

The fabulous earnings of movie stars became part of their public image, raised them high above the level of mere wage earners, placed them in some never-never land where all sorts of wondrous things were happening. Hollywood, the capital of the movie industry, became a Camelot, a legendary place where men and women, beautiful beyond the dreams of ordinary mortals, always wrapped in costly furs and bespangled with diamonds, spend their lives in leisurely pursuits, the chief of them being lovemaking. All the technical devices of the industry were mobilized to create and enhance that image; in the films of the thirties a kind of lighting was used which bathed the screen in a silvery glow, creating haloes around the heads of the stars. George Hurrell, the master portrait photographer, charged the studios $1,000 a sitting (in the thirties!) to produce those superglamourous photographs which were collected by fans throughout the world.

Blinded by all that glamour radiating from the film world and by the phenomenal earnings of the stars, the public did not realize that being in films paid those actors fortunate enough to have jobs very poorly. A 1977 survey conducted under the auspices of the U.S. Department of Labor disclosed that 23 percent of the members of the Screen Actors Guild had annual incomes below $7,000, which enabled them to qualify for welfare assistance.

The rise of the movie actor also enhanced the image of the actor as the embodiment of sexual attractiveness and as a practitioner of licentious sex; in addition, it blurred to the point of disappearance the line separating the roles played by the actor from his private life.

"The cinema, that temple of sex with its goddesses, its guardians, and its victims,"[13] exulted Jean Cocteau. The sex goddess appeared at the very beginning of the film era. The first of them, Theda Bara, appeared in 1915 in a film entitled *A Fool There Was*, portraying a malevolent temptress whose charms were as irresistible as they were fatal to hapless men.

Theda Bara was the invention of William Fox, the pioneer image maker. Under his ministrations, a girl named Theodosia Goodman, the daughter of a Cincinnati tailor, became transmogrified into an Egyptian, born to a fabulously rich sheikh, the mistress of a succession of Bedouin princes, introduced into the mysteries of love by witches, skilled in the art of distilling perfumes which drove men crazy with desire.

In 1915 the movie-going public was new to all this, and capable of swallowing any garbage shovelled by the studios. The star appeared at press conferences held in a hotel room decorated to look like a luxurious tent, the air heavy with incense. In his "Upton

Sinclair Presents William Fox," the writer reports on one of those press conferences. He had lingered after the other reporters left and he saw Theda Bara, who had pretended not to know English and communicated with the reporters through an interpreter, jump off the couch on which she was reclining and run to the window shouting "Gimme some air!"[14]

Theda Bara was followed by a long succession of sex goddesses. None of the build-ups that followed was as crude as hers, but all were based on the extraordinary—almost supernatural—sexual attractiveness of the star, and the star's screen persona was extended to cover her private life.

The sexual build-up was to a great degree based on fetishism. There was the platinum-blond hair of Jean Harlow (in a fit of rage at being so cynically exploited by the studio, the actress once hacked off her famous hair, and for weeks after had to wear a wig), who would rub her nipples with ice cubes before press conferences, so that they should expand in the heat of the room to the delight of reporters; there was Mae West with her padded hips, the mistress of the sexual innuendo (in *I Am No Angel* we see an elderly man leaving her apartment, and trying to shake her hand misses the target. "I see you have trouble with your hand too, Judge,"[15] she remarks in an off-hand manner); producer Howard Hughes carried out a multi-million-dollar promotion campaign on behalf of Jane Russell, the campaign based solely on the actress's extraordinarily large breasts—her only asset.

More sophisticated than Hollywood, the French movie industry came up with a sex queen to top all American products. The sixties saw the phenomenon of Brigitte Bardot, a sex machine on the screen and in her well-publicized, minutely reported private life. Superbly endowed by nature, she topped her face with a mass of tangled hair, suggestive of wild tussles in bed. American movie critic Dwight McDonald thus described, perhaps with a touch of national envy, the star's appearance: "Bardot has become a grotesque, a product of biological overspecialization, like a borzoi; her face has been reduced to the sexual essentials and is, objectively considered, by now rather terrifying . . . those huge staring eyes, the great thick-lipped toothy mouth, the cascades and whorls and fountains of yellow hair, like a witchdoctor's get up."[16]

The marital and extramarital adventures of the idols of the screen have become part of the global folklore of the twentieth century, cultivated by the press and other media, with the idols all too eager to cooperate. A Hollywood reporter went through the trouble of compiling the statements to the press issued by Elizabeth Taylor on the occasion of some of her marriages:

I am now Mrs. Hilton. You can take it from me that my romantic life is settled forever. There is no other future for me than as Nicky's wife.

It is wonderful marrying a man like Michael who is twice my age. He is so mature and that is what I need.

I have given Mike my love, my eternal love.

I love Eddie dearly.

Richard, unless he wants to divorce me, will never be divorced by me.[17]

The movie star's public image is a precious commodity, a property in which the studios invested large sums of money. The star thus becomes wedded to that image; a deviation is bound to have dire results for the person and the studio.

Elizabeth Taylor was built up as the spoiled, rich, talented girl with the body of a woman and the mind of a child. The public expected of her and enjoyed her marital tangles; each divorce and marriage enhanced her public appeal, and was followed by increases in her earnings.

On the other hand, the romance of Swedish Ingrid Bergman with her Italian director Roberto Rossellini in the fifties became a public scandal, and all but ruined the actress's career. This was because she had been built up as the wholesome, unspoiled child of the North, happily living with her physician husband when not in Hollywood making a picture. When the news came out that she had set up illicit housekeeping with Rossellini, the public felt cheated. In order to save its investment, the studio had to start from scratch to build a new image. A Fox executive frankly stated that they would have to "convince the public that she was a courageous, long suffering woman who had sacrificed all for love."[18]

Another example is the hero of a novel set in the movie world who is ordered by the studio boss to abandon the woman he loves, who is about to bear his illegitimate child. The studio publicity people spend a little fortune on bribes to keep the affair from being splashed across newspaper pages because his entanglement would interfere with the character he plays in an about-to-be-released movie. The boss's irresistible argument is that, in return for the huge fee paid to the actor, he is expected to show some coopera-tion.[19]

The advent of the movies as the most popular medium of enter-tainment has also contributed to the widespread notion that there is really little to the art of the actor, if it is an art at all. Admittedly, it takes considerably less acting talent to be successful in the movies than on the live stage, the movie actor's performance as seen by the public being the end product of the joint efforts of actor, director, cameraman, make-up artist, lighting designer, and film editor. Stars such as Hedy Lamarr, Lana Turner, and Robert Taylor made their way more on the strength of their looks, sex appeal, and what goes under the name of personality than on the strength of their acting ability. Humphrey Bogart, one of the few Hollywood actors who came to the screen after years on the stage, had an exceedingly poor opinion of his film colleagues. "It's unusual to get a trained actor out here," he was quoted. "Most of these young glamor boys in the movies today used to work as gas station attendants. They aren't actors. Go into any major studio and shout 'Fill her up' and all the leading men in the place will come instinctively running."[20]

The sexual role of the actor underwent considerable change as a result of the sexual revolution and the new permissiveness. For the first time in the history of the theatre—the crudest type of the late-Roman spectacles and the backstreet illegal theatres of modern times excepted—full nudity and even simulated sex were being shown on the stage in plays by reputable playwrights, with repu-table actors performing.

One of the first to take advantage of the new freedom was the New York Living Theatre. Radically departing from practically every theatrical tradition, the Living Theatre staged in the sixties a number of shows where the barrier between the audience and stage disappeared, as did the separation between reality and fiction. In the play *The Connection*, which dealt with drug addition, real drug addicts performed and they solicited handouts from the audience during intermission. The company also refused to pay taxes, and when the taxmen came to dispossess them, they staged a sit-in strike which was in fact an improvised performance—for an audience.

The company's avowed purpose, in the words of its founders Julian Beck and Judith Malina, was "the exteriorization of the interior scream," by means of yoga trances, grunts, groans, howls, mad choreography. Sexual expression was given free reign, as frenzied naked bodies whirled on the stage, often joined by members of the audience.

True to their principles, the Living Theatre actors acted off stage as they did in the theatre. When they were giving guest performances in New Haven, several of them were arrested for walking in the street naked.

While stage nudity for the Living Theatre was an expression of the company's philosophy, of the belief that sexual freedom was necessary for the radical social change they advocated, frontal nudity and simulated sex in a play like Peter Shaffer's *Equus* were simply acts of stage realism, made possible by the changed attitude of the public.

Then came the expected exploitation of the new freedom. One of the trail blazers was *Oh Calcutta!*, conceived by the British critic Kenneth Tynan, a semipoetic, semipornographic revue in which all performers, male and female, appeared stark naked. It became a popular success around the world, while most critics saw in the show little more than a joke and titillation of the audience.

Stage nudity naturally added a new element to the profession of acting. The actor, who by the very nature of his calling nightly exposes himself to the public, this time did so fully and literally, and his image as a practitioner of licentious sex received added confirmation. Nudity also created new problems in the profession. Actors' unions began to demand that "escape clauses" be inserted in contracts for cases when an actor hired for a part learns that he or she is to appear nude, and is not inclined to do so.

It was more a problem of economics than of morale. In view of the employment situation in the profession, one had to have very grave objections to appearing nude in order to refuse a part. An actor would not only miss the chance of working, but frequently he would forfeit his chances of ever working again for a certain director or company. In 1970 in England, an actress worked an average of fourteen weeks a year, earning an average of £450. Under those circumstances it was difficult indeed to refuse any job. An official of British Equity stated it in clear terms: "It is not nudity that is the issue—it is not up to Equity to pass moral judgments—but the difficulties caused by underemployment."[21]

In December 1970, British Equity published an article by a member under the title "Is Nudity Good for Our Business?" The author of the article found nudity demeaning to the actor, and blamed his colleagues for its spread. "Who is partly to blame for this? We are! Because it would seem that some of us will do anything to see our name in lights, anything for money. We will allow managers to desecrate our dignity, and, at the same time, encourage audiences who should be worthy of better things, to become nothing more than a pack of raincoated voyeurs."[22]

Not all actors felt that appearing nude was demeaning. A woman who was auditioned for a part in *Oh Calcutta!* was exhilarated by the experience. As she told an interviewer,

> I had never taken off my clothes in public before. And after it was all over, and I'd put my clothes back on, Jacques Levy, the director, asked me, "Well, how do you feel?" I was beaming and I said "Fantastic! I feel fantastic!" I gave him a big hug and a kiss and I thanked him. There was something so fantastic about—not about exhibiting my body—but being *able* to. It was a very free feeling. I came out of the audition room and all the others were out there being very nervous, and I said "it's fantastic, you'll love it!"[23]

In the mid-seventies simulated sexual intercourse was no longer a rarity on the stage, and although no cases of nonsimulated sex on legitimate stages were known, the possibility of it happening was sufficient for the American Equity to inform its members in a circular that should anyone be arrested for performing such an act on the stage, the organization would not provide the actor or actress with legal aid.

In 1977, a sensational trial took place in Munich. Ingrid Van Bergen, a beautiful, highly successful stage, film, and television actress, was charged with the murder, in a state of drunkenness, of her unfaithful lover, a well-known local playboy. Trying to soften the hearts of the judges, the actress's defending attorney argued: "Actors and actresses are special people. The theatre is another world. Sexuality and eroticism play a great role in their lives. So does alcohol. Actors and actresses often perform in real life their roles on the stage.''[24] Or, as Plato said twenty-four centuries earlier, ''The mask they wear may become their face.''

NOTES

1. *Canadian Theatre Review* (Summer 1968), p. 35.

2. International Theatre Institute, *Informations* (Autumn 1976), p. 26.

3. Jennifer Merin, ''Just an Actor,'' *Canadian Theatre Review* (Summer 1977), pp. 145-53.

4. Jennifer Merin, ''Just An Actor,'' *Canadian Theatre Review* (Spring 1978), p. 138.

5. Tallulah Bankhead, *Tallulah: An Autobiography of Tallulah Bankhead* (New York: Harper & Row, 1952), pp. 320-21.

6. Marian Seldes, *The Bright Lights* (Boston: Houghton Mifflin, 1978), p. 233.

7. Len Deighton, *Close Up* (London: Jonathan Cape, 1972), p. 35.

8. Ronald Hayman, *The Set Up: An Anatomy of the English Theatre Today* (London: Eyre Methuen, 1973), p. 49.

9. Jennifer Merin, ''Just an Actor,'' *Canadian Theatre Review* (Summer 1978), pp. 116-17.

10. Faubion Bowers, *Broadway USSR* (New York: Thomas Nelson & Sons, 1959), pp. 144-45.

11. Bankhead, *Tallulah*, pp. 320-21.

12. George Bernard Shaw, *Shaw on Theatre*, ed. E. J. West (New York: Hill & Wang, 1958), p. 189.

13. Alexander Walker, *Sex in the Movies* (Harmondsworth, Eng.: Penguin Books, 1968), preface.

14. Ibid., p. 25.

15. Ibid., p. 75.

16. Dwight MacDonald, *On Movies* (Englewood Cliffs, N.J.: Prentice-Hall, 1969), p. 443.

17. John Cottrell and Fergus Cashin, *Richard Burton* (London: Coronet Books, Hodder Paperbacks, 1974), pp. 233-34.

18. Walker, *Sex in the Movies*, p. 147.

19. Deighton, *Close Up*, p. 290.

20. Cottrell and Cashin, *Richard Burton*, p. 154.

21. Jann Perry, ''To Strip or Not,'' *New Society*, 10 December 1970, p. 1050.

22. Ibid.

23. n.a., *On the Theatre*, p. 316.

24. *Time*, 8 August 1977.

Bibliography

Baker, Michael. *The Rise of the Victorian Actor*. London: Rowman, Little-field, 1978.

Bankhead, Tallulah. *Tallulah: An Autobiography of Tallulah Bankhead*. New York: Harper & Row, 1952.

Barras, Moses. *The Stage Controversy in France from Corneille to Rousseau*. New York: Phaeton, 1973.

Bowers, Faubion. *Broadway USSR*. New York: Thomas Nelson & Sons, 1959.

Bradbrook, M. C. *The Rise of the Common Player*. Cambridge: Harvard University Press, 1962.

Buckingham, J. S. *America: Historical, Statistic and Descriptive*. London: Fisher & Co., 1940.

Carroll, David. *The Matinee Idols*. London: Peter Owen, 1973.

Chambers, Edmund K. *The Medieval Stage*. Vol. 1. London: Oxford University Press, 1903.

_____. *The Elizabethan Stage*. Vol. 4. London: Oxford University Press, 1923.

Cibber, Colley. *An Apology for the Life of Colley Cibber*. London: J. M. Dent & Sons, 1914.

Cicero, Marcus Tullius. *De Republica*. Cambridge: Harvard University Press, Loeb Classical Library, 1931.

_____. *Speeches*. Cambridge: Harvard University Press, Loeb Classical Library, 1931.

Cole, Toby, and Helen Krich Chinoy. *Actors on Acting*. New York: Crown, 1970.

Collier, Jeremy. *A Short View of the Immorality, & Profaneness of the English Stage* New York: Garland, 1972.

_____. *Collier Tracts: 1703-1708*. New York: Garland, 1973.

Collins, Herbert. *Talma.* New York: Hill & Wang, 1964.

Cottrell, John, and Fergus Cashin. *Richard Burton.* London: Coronet Books, Hodder Paperbacks, 1974.

Deighton, Len. *Close Up.* London: Jonathan Cape, 1972.

Downer, Alan S. *The Eminent Tragedian: William Charles Macready.* Cambridge: Harvard University Press, 1966.

Dunlap, William. *A History of the American Theatre.* New York: Burt Franklin, 1963.

Duvignaud, Jean. *L'Acteur: Esquisse d'une Sociologie du Comédien.* Paris: Editions Gallimard, 1965.

Elsom, John. *The Erotic Theatre.* London: Secker & Warburg, 1973.

Evelyn, John. *The Diary of John Evelyn.* Edited by E. S. De Baer. London: Oxford University Press, Clarendon Press, 1955.

Fenichel, Otto. "On Acting." *Psychoanalytic Quarterly* 15, no. 2 (1946).

Freud, Sigmund. *The Basic Writings of Sigmund Freud.* Translated and edited by Abraham A. Brill. New York: Random House, Modern Library, 1938.

Friedlander, Ludwig. *Roman Life and Manners under the Early Empire.* London: Routledge & Kegan Paul, 1965.

Furnas, J. C. *The Americans: A Social History of the United States, 1587-1914.* New York: G. P. Putnam & Sons, 1969.

Germain, Jean-Claude. "Théâtre Quebeçois or Theatre Protestant?" *Canadian Theatre Review,* Summer 1976.

Gilder, Rosamond. *Enter the Actress: The First Woman in the Theatre.* New York: Theatre Arts Books, 1959.

Gray, Charles Harold. *Theatrical Criticism in London to 1795.* New York: Benjamin Bloom, 1964.

Hayman, Ronald. *The Set Up: An Anatomy of the English Theatre Today.* London: Eyre Methuen, 1973.

Heiko, Juergens. *Pompa Diaboli.* Berlin: Verlag Hohlammer, 1972.

Heywood, Thomas. *An Apology for Actors* (1612). New York: Garland, 1973.

Hornblow, Arthur. *A History of the Theatre in America.* Vol. 1, *From the Beginning to the Civil War.* New York: Benjamin Bloom, 1919.

Hotson, Leslie. *The Commonwealth and Restoration Stage.* Cambridge: Harvard University Press, 1928.

Howe, Irving. *The World of Our Fathers.* New York: Harcourt Brace Jovanovich, 1976.

Irving, Laurence. *Henry Irving: The Actor and His World.* London: Faber & Faber, 1951.

Kimmel, Stanley. *The Mad Booths of Maryland.* New York: Bobbs Merrill Co., 1940.

Kinderman, Heinz. *Theatregeschichte Europas.* Vol. 1. Salzburg: O. Müller, 1957.

Larroumet, Gustave. "Revue de G. Mangras, *Les Comédiens hors la loi.*" *Revue Politique et Littéraire.* 22 October 1887.

Lucian of Samosata. *Of Pantomine* in his *Dialogues.* 8 vols. Cambridge: Harvard University Press, Loeb Classical Library, 1931.

McAfee, Helen. *Pepys on the Restoration Stage.* New York: Benjamin Bloom, 1916.

McCollum, John, ed. *The Restoration Stage.* Westport, Conn.: Greenwood Press, 1973.

MacDonald, Dwight. *On Movies.* Englewood Cliffs, N.J.: Prentice-Hall, 1969.

Macready, William Charles. *The Diaries of William Charles Macready, 1832-1851.* Edited by J. C. Trewin. London: Longmans, Green & Co., 1967.

Mantzius, Karl. *A History of Theatrical Art in Ancient and Modern Times.* Vols. 1, 4, 5, 6. Translated by Louise von Cossel. New York: Peter Smith, 1937.

Maugham, Somerset. *The Summing Up.* London: William Heinemann, 1948.

Merin, Jennifer. "Just an Actor." *Canadian Theatre Review.* Summer 1977, Spring and Summer 1978.

Moody, Richard. *Edwin Forrest.* New York: Alfred A. Knopf, 1960.

————. "American Actors, Managers, Producers and Directors" in *American Drama.* Edited by Travis Bogard, Richard Moody and Walter J. Meserve. Vol. 8. *The Revels History of Drama in English.* London: Barnes and Noble, 1977.

Nagler, A. M. *A Source Book in Theatrical History.* New York: Dover, 1952.

Nepos, Cornelius. *Praefatio.* Cambridge: Harvard University Press, Loeb Classical Library, 1931.

Nicoll, Allardyce. *Masks, Mimes, and Miracles.* London: Harrap & Co., 1930.

Pickard-Cambridge, Sir Arthur. *The Dramatic Festivals of Athens.* London: Oxford University Press, 1933.

Playfair, Giles. *Kean: The Life and Paradox of the Great Actor.* London: Reinhardt & Evans, 1950.

Price, Cecil. *Theatre in the Age of Garrick.* Oxford: Basil Blackwell, 1973.

Racine, Jean. *Phèdre* from *The Complete Plays of Jean Racine.* Vol. 2. Translated by Samuel Solomon. New York: Random House, 1967.

Rankin, Hugh. *The Theatre in Colonial America.* Chapel Hill: University of North Carolina Press, 1965.

Rennert, Hugo Albert. *The Spanish Stage of the Times of Lope de Vega.* New York: Hispanic Society of America, 1909.

Richardson, Joanna. *La Vie Parisienne.* New York: Viking Press, 1971.

_____. *The Courtesans: The Demi-monde in Nineteenth Century France.* London: Weidenfeld & Nicolson, 1967.

Rousseau, Jean-Jacques. *Politics and the Arts: Letter to M. D'Alembert on the Theatre.* Translated with notes and introduction by Allan Bloom. Glencoe, Ill.: Free Press, 1960.

Sachs, Arieh. *Shkiyat Haletzan* (The Prankster's Decline). Vol. 5, proceedings of the Israel National Academy of Sciences, 1978.

Seldes, Marian. *The Bright Lights.* Boston: Houghton Mifflin, 1978.

Shaw, George Bernard. *Shaw on Theatre.* Edited by E. J. West. New York: Hill & Wang, 1958.

Shergold, N. D. *A History of the Spanish Theatre.* London: Oxford University Press, Clarendon Press, 1967.

Smith, Winifred. *Italian Actors of the Renaissance.* New York: Coward McCann, 1930.

Taubman, Howard. *The Making of the American Theatre.* New York: Coward McCann, 1965.

Tertullian. *Di Spectaculis.* Cambridge: Harvard University Press, Loeb Classical Library, 1931.

Trewin, J. C., ed. *Theatre Bedside Book: An Anthology of the Stage.* Newton Abbott, Eng.: David & Charles, 1974.

Varneke, B. V. *A History of the Russian Theatre: Seventeenth through Nineteenth Centuries.* New York: Hafner Press, 1971.

Walker, Alexander, *Sex in the Movies.* Harmondsworth, Eng.: Penguin Books, 1968.

Wiedenfeld, Dieter. *Der Schauspieler un der Gesellschaft.* Cologne: Deutsche Artze Verlag GmbH, 1959.

Wiley, W. L. *The Early Public Theatre in France.* Cambridge: Harvard University Press, 1909.

Index

Grattan, Thomas Colley (*Ben Nazir*),
129
Greek comedy, in ancient Rome, 24-25
Greek theatre, classical, 13-19
Greek tragedy, in ancient Rome, 25
Greene, Robert, 61, 63-64, 65
*Greene's Groat's-Worth of Wit bought
with a Million of Repentance*
(Greene), 64
Grigori, Johann Gottfried, 100
Gwynn, Nell, 72-73, 75

Hallam, Adam, 141
Hallam, Lewis, 141, 142
Hallam Company, 141-42
The Hamburg Dramaturgy (Lessing), 97
Hamburg National Theatre, 97
Hamlet (Shakespeare), 146
Hanswurst, 93-94, 99
Harlow, Jean, 174
Hazlitt, William, 121, 122
Heliogabalus, Emperor, 21
Hernani (Hugo), 117
Heywood, Thomas (*Apology for
Actors*), 7, 61-62
Hiffernan, Paul, 92
Hilarius, Bishop of Arles, 27
Hodgson, Captain, 76
Hoffman, E.T.A., 119
Hollywood, 172-73
Hôtel de Bourgogne, 50, 52
Houghton, Lord, 151
Howe, Irving (*World of Our Fathers*),
10
Hughes, Howard, 174
Hugo, Victor (*Hernani*), 117
Hurrell, George, 173
Hylas, 20

I Am No Angel, 174
Ibsen, Henrik, 161
Illusion in theatre, power of, 3-4
Income of actors: in ancient Greece,
17; in 18th century, 82; in Elizabethan England, 58, 65; of movie
actors, 172-73; in Russia, 102, 133;

of Shakespeare, 64; in 20th century,
166-73; in United States, 136
Independent Theatre, 161
Industrial Revolution, 152
Inn yards, stages in, 58
Irish Literary Theatre, 161
Irving, Henry (John Brodribb), 5, 7,
150-51
Irving, Laurence, 151
Irving, Washington, 142-43
Italian theatre: actresses in, 10; income
of actors in, 167; Renaissance, 39-45

Jaegermann, Frau, 99
James, Henry, 154
Jesters, 9
The Jew, 60
John Chrysostom, Saint, 32
Johnson, Samuel, 82
Jonson, Ben, 65
Judaism, and theatre, 9
Judson, E.Z.C. (Ned Buntline), 148
Justinian II, Emperor, 28

Kallipides, 16
Karatygin, A. P., 133
Karatygin, Wassily Andreyevich, 133
Kean, Edmund, 92, 120-21, 122-29, 143
Kean, Thomas, 139
Kemble, John Philip, 92, 93, 121-22
Kemble, Sarah (Mrs. Siddons), 92-93
Kendal, Margaret, 155
Killigrew, Thomas, 69
Kimmel, Stanley, 144
King Lear (Shakespeare), 120
Kohansky, Mendel, ix

Lamarr, Hedy, 176
Lamb, Charles, 61
Laporte (Mathieu Le Fèbvre), 50-51
Lauredus, 21
Laval, P. A., 114-15
Le Boeuf, Jean-Jacques, 115
Lecouvreur, Adrienne, 82, 83, 84-85, 87
Le Fèbvre, Mathieu (Laporte), 50-51
Legrand, 84

About the Author

MENDEL KOHANSKY was the theatre critic of the *Jerusalem Post* from 1961 until his death in May of 1982. A noted writer, critic, and authority on the Israeli theatre, he contributed to many important volumes on the theatre including *The Oxford Companion to the Theatre, Der Schauspielführer, Encyclopedia Judaica, The Hebrew Encyclopedia*, the new edition of the *McGraw Hill Encyclopedia of World Drama*, and *Teatro del Novocento*. He was the author of *The Hebrew Theatre, Its First Fifty Years*, the first and most comprehensive book on the subject. His other works included *Mirror to Death*, a book on the Holocaust as the theme in world drama; *The Wiedenfeld Guide to Israel—Tel Aviv and Environs*; and a monograph on the sculptor Eli Ilan. Mr. Kohansky's articles on theatre and the arts appeared in publications in Britain, Canada, Israel, Italy, and the United States.